The
SANSKRIT ALPHABET
with
VEDIC EXTENSIONS

Ashwini Kumar Aggarwal

जय गुरुदेव

ISBN13: 978-81-950754-0-9 Paperback Edition
ISBN13: 978-81-950754-1-6 Hardbound Edition
ISBN13: 978-81-950754-9-2 Digital Edition

Title: The Sanskrit Alphabet with Vedic Extensions
Author: Ashwini Kumar Aggarwal

Printed and Published by
Devotees of Sri Sri Ravi Shankar Ashram
34 Sunny Enclave, Devigarh Road,
Patiala 147001, Punjab, India

https://advaita56.weebly.com/
The Art of Living Centre

https://www.artofliving.org/

15th January 2021, Plaza Rudra Puja and School Foundation Stone

Pausha Shukla Paksha Dvitiya, Shatabhisha Nakshatra, Uttarayana

Vikram Samvat 2077 Pramadi, Saka Era 1942 Sharvari

1st Edition January 2021

जय गुरुदेव

Gurudev Sri Sri Ravi Shankar
Our path giver

An offering at His Lotus feet

जय गुरुदेव

This book arose out of the adventures faced in typing Sanskrit on the computer.

When we used to write Sanskrit in school then it was quite easy as we could form any letter of our choice as per need in constructing a sentence.

However, the challenge surfaced when interest arose in putting the knowledge gained into print. Most word processors either lacked the font glyphs or it was difficult to ascertain how to correctly type a particular character.

Since the scriptures were handed down in an oral tradition, most of the sounds were never written but only spoken! The system of writing developed rather recently and is still undergoing change. There are variations in notations, character usage and spelling in the various printed texts.

In English texts, there is always a tendency to spell a Sanskrit word without the ending visarga or the makara, or in its stem form. Here also a strict Sanskrit spelling in first case प्रथमा विभक्ति or in बहुवचन has not been adhered to, to keep the text light and lively.

A reasonable level of fluency having been attained in Sanskrit; this book has been written to share the knowledge for common benefit.

While reading Vedic Texts, we notice some letters, characters and symbols that are in addition to the Sanskrit Alphabet given. These characters are the chanting pitch or tone accent marks, additional letters and punctuations, and are found in Vedic Sanskrit literature.

संस्कृत को देवों की भाषा कहा गया । संस्कृत में ही वेदों का बखान हुआ । उपनिषद का उल्लेख हो, या कालिदास की 'उट्र से लेकर उष्ट्र' तक की यात्रा, महाभारत का हृदय विदारक वर्णन हो या गीता का ज्ञान, गुरु–शिष्य की गूढ़ वार्ता हो या माँ दुर्गा की स्तुति, संस्कृत के बिना तो कुछ भी अभिव्यक्त न हुआ ।

आदिकाल में एकमात्र संस्कृत भाषा का ही आधिपत्य था, जिसने प्रत्येक कवि, लेखक, साहित्यकार, शैलीकार या कहानीकार की लेखनी से न केवल अभिव्यक्ति पाई, वरन उससे असीम सफलता भी पाई । आधुनिक युग की भी हर भाषा व लिपि का मूल संस्कृत में ही तो है ।
Australia originated from 'अष्ट्र + आलय', the twelve months January to December find their roots and meaning in Sanskrit.

आज के वैज्ञानिकों ने भी अपनी शोध (research) के द्वारा संस्कृत के उच्चारण व पठन–पाठन से मन मस्तिष्क पर पड़ने वाले सकारात्म प्रभावों को देखा, परखा और अनुमोदित (recommend) किया है । इसीलिए मात्र भारतवर्ष ही नहीं अपितु भौतिक साधनों में अग्रणी पाश्चात्य देशों में भी संस्कृत की शिक्षा–दीक्षा को प्राथमिक शिक्षा स्तर पर ही अनिवार्य करने की जागरूकता आई है ।

'The Sanskrit Alphabet' is one of the most basic, essential yet most profound work in the direction of making Sanskrit learning, reading, writing, and typing with keyboard, not only possible but effective and efficient.

इस मूलभूत प्रयास से आज की पीढ़ी भी आसानी से जान सकेगी संस्कृत को । यह प्रयास एक कड़ी की भांति जोड़ सकेगा आधुनिक पीढ़ी को वैदिक ज्ञान–कोष की जड़ो से, और सशक्त सांस्कृतिक धरोहरों से, वह भी समकालीन प्रौद्योगिकी व तकनीकी ज्ञान के साथ साथ ।

मैं हृदय से आभार व्यक्त करती हूँ और साधुवाद देती हूँ श्रीमान अश्विनी अग्रवाल जी को, इस सोच के लिए तथा उन अथक प्रयासों के लिए जिनके फलस्वरूप यह पुस्तक इस मूर्त रूप में आई । बधाई अर्पित है प्रेरणास्रोत, ज्ञान मूर्ति गुरुदेव के चरण कमलों में ।

इस पुस्तक में अनिवार्य ज्ञान को सरल, क्रमबद्ध व सुनियोजित प्रकार से इस भांति लिखा गया है कि हर स्तर के (प्रारम्भिक, नौसिखिए, या विशेषज्ञ) पाठकों को अनिवार्य मार्गदर्शन के साथ साथ प्रेरणा भी मिलेगी ।

शुभेच्छाओं के साथ

May 01, 2017

(Dr. Seema Bawa)
Professor, Comp. Sc. & Engg.

Ex–Dean (Student Affairs)

Ex–Head (Comp. Sc. & Engg.)
Professor In-Charge Nava Nalanda Central Library
Thapar Institute of Engineering and Technology, Patiala

Table of Contents

Blessing

Let us do the आ Meditation. Notice that as you chant mentally, the sound never dies. You can chant eternally. The Sanskrit word for alphabet is अक्षर । न क्षरति इति अक्षर । That which has no decay is called the Alphabet.

H H Sri Sri Ravi Shankar
5th February 2017, Gita Ek Samvaad, New Delhi

Table of Manuscript Text Plates

Introduction

The Sanskrit Alphabet वर्णमाला consists of 56 letters.
vowels स्वर - 20 (popular tradition lists 13, without pluta vowels)
consonants व्यञ्जन - 34 (popular tradition lists 33, without ळ)
anusvara and visarga – 2 (there are 4 additional vedic ayogavahas)

a written consonant क is usually supplied with the vowel अ for purpose of enunciation . without a vowel, the हलन्त symbol is used to write a consonant. Actual consonant should be with a halant e.g. क् Such a consonant is technically termed a half-letter.

the ह is an aspirate, i.e. mahaprana. it is named thus.
the hakara is also an exception when writing conjuncts. संयुक्त अक्षर

Anusvara and Candrabindu

An anusvara ं is a nasal नासिका । uttered with mouth closed and emphasis on the nose. usually pronounced as म्
The candrabindu ँ is an anunasika अनुनासिका । uttered from the mouth with emphasis on the nose. pronounced as न् or म्

the jihvamuliya ✕ is a guttural visarga

the upadhmaniya ✕ or ⚹ is a labial visarga

Avagraha ऽ denotes the elision of अ आ to prevent loss of meaning.
ळ is usually found in Vedic texts and rarely in classical sanskrit.

Sanskrit numerals combine like the English numerals in number representation, viz. units, decimals, thousands, etc.

This work is relevant both for the western reader as well as the Indian audience. The usage of diacritics is kept to a minimum. Enjoy exploring the letters and sounds that have found a place in all the languages of the world.

The Sanskrit Alphabet

संस्कृत वर्णमाला

अ आ इ ई उ ऊ ऋ ॠ ऌ ॡ   ए ऐ ओ औ   अं अः   अँ

					The Shiva Sounds
क्	ख्	ग्	घ्	ङ्	
च्	छ्	ज्	झ्	ञ्	
ट्	ठ्	ड्	ढ्	ण्	The Brahma Sounds
त्	थ्	द्	ध्	न्	
प्	फ्	ब्	भ्	म्	The Vishnu Sounds
य् र् ल् व्		श् ष् स्		ह्	
		ळ्	व्ह्		Vedic Sanskrit
० १ २ ३ ४ ५ ६ ७ ८ ९					Numerals
क्ष ज्ञ श्र					Conjunct letter

Additional letters found in Vedic Sanskrit are ळ॰ and व्ह ।
The consonant ळ॰ is an alternate version of ड॰ alpaprana usage.

अग्निमीडे -> अग्निमीळे agnimīḍe -> agnimīḻe

अग्निम् ईडे Agni (is to be) praised. ई ड् ए -> ई ळ् ए Rigveda 1.1.1

Likewise व्ह replaces ढ in mahaprana usage.

दृढं -> दृळ्हं dṛḍhaṁ -> dṛ̱ḻhaṁ दृ ढ् अं -> दृ व्ह अं Rigveda 4.1.1

The vowel long ॡ is not found in literature. It is given only in the
alphabet, grammar books or in font sets. Hence crossed out.

Font glyph variations in some old Sanskrit texts

अ ऄ , आ ऑ , ओ ओ ,औ औ , झ झ , ण ण

Conjunct letter संयुक्त अक्षर
क्ष ज्ञ श्र are not letters of the alphabet. Rather these are conjuncts
that have become popular in writing. An earlier form of क्ष is क्त ।

Characteristics of Letters

In the Sanskrit Alphabet, the letters have distinct characteristics.

Simple Vowels - अ आ इ ई उ ऊ ऋ ॠ ऌ
>> Short Vowels ह्रस्व - अ इ उ ऋ ऌ called लघु स्वर light syllable
>> Long Vowels दीर्घ - आ ई ऊ ॠ
>> Conjunct Vowels - ऋ (अर्) ॠ (आर्) ऌ (अल्)

Diphthong Vowels - ए ऐ ओ औ
>> Vowel compounds - ए (अ इ) ऐ (आ इ) ओ (अ उ) औ (आ उ)
>> Also known as गुरु स्वर heavy syllable

Ayogavaha अयोगवाह Sounds - अनुस्वार अं , विसर्जनीय अः , चंद्रबिंदु अँ

Row class consonants

क् ख् ग् घ् ङ्   च् छ् ज् झ् ञ्   ट् ठ् ड् ढ् ण्   त् थ् द् ध् न्   प् फ् ब् भ् म्

Semivowels अन्तःस्थ midway between vowel and consonant य् र् ल् व्

Sibilants ऊष्म - श् ष् स्

Aspirate ऊष्म तथा महाप्राण – ह्

Vedic Sandhi letters ळ् , व्ह्

Vedic Ayogavaha Sounds अᳵ, अᳶ, ᳱ (गुँ , गं᳴), ᳲ, हुँ, र्, य

Numerals are combined just as in English to form succeeding numbers, e.g. १० ११ १२ ५०१ ८५६७

Alphabet as Commonly Written

The Sanskrit alphabet is commonly written without a halant. Consonants cannot be uttered without a vowel. So in teaching, each consonant is supplied with the vowel अ , so that it can be uttered. Here are the 56 letters of the classical Sanskrit Alphabet.

20 Vowels

अ आ अ३ इ ई इ३ उ ऊ उ३ ऋ ॠ ऋ३ ऌ ऌ३ ए ऐ ए३ ओ औ ओ३

34 Consonants

क	ख	ग	घ	ङ
च	छ	ज	झ	ञ
ट	ठ	ड	ढ	ण
त	थ	द	ध	न
प	फ	ब	भ	म

य र ल व

श ष स   ह

ळ

2 Ayogavahas

अं अः

Vowels
अआ इई उऊ ऋॠ लृ एऐ ओऔ अं अः

Consonants

क	ख	ग	घ	ङ
च	छ	ज	झ	ञ
ट	ठ	ड	ढ	ण
त	थ	द	ध	न
प	फ	ब	भ	म

य र ल व

श ष स ह

Grammar schools usually teach it like this.

Unicodes for Letters

The Unicode consortium has fixed the alphanumeric hex codes so that there is uniformity across devices and operating systems in typing the letters. For Devanagari script letters, the unicodes go from 0900 to 097F. Rather easy to remember because India's country code for international phone dialling is +91.

In case one has forgotten hex coding, no matter. Decimal numbers go from 0 to 9, i.e. ten digits, and then combine to make 10, 11 etc. Similarly, hex numbers go from 0 to 9 then A B C D E F, i.e. 16 digits, then combine to make 10, 11, 12, 13, 14, 15, 16, 17, 18, 19, 1A, 1B, 1C, 1D, 1E, 1F, 20, 21, etc.

The online charts for Unicodes are available at
http://www.unicode.org/charts/#scripts
The unicodes relevant for Sanskrit are in the three different charts named Devanagari, Devanagari Extended and Vedic Extensions.

More resources
http://www.unicode.org/faq/indic.html
http://www.unicode.org/resources/keyboards.html
http://www.unicode.org/resources/fonts.html
http://www.unicode.org/resources/online-tools.html

अ 0905 आ 0906 etc. These letters are easy to enter on a computer. However, we may find it difficult to type the special letters, so some of these are listed. To type any of these characters, simply enter the unicode and then press **ALT+x** keys on a windows computer.

E.g. to type ॐ, type 0950 **ALT+x** and the symbol ॐ appears, if the relevant font is installed in your machine.

अँ 0901	ळ 0933	ऽ 093D	ॠ 0908	ॡ 0960	ऌ 090C	् 094D
ॐ 0950	꣠ 094E	॰ 0970	ृ 0943	ॄ 0944	ॢ 0962	0971
़ 093C	ड़ 095C	ढ़ 095D	ज़ 095B	॑ 0951	॒ 0952	᳚ 1CDA
। 0964	॥ 0965	य़ 097A	ᳲ 1CF2	A8F2	ꣳ A8F3	ꣴ A8F4
᳭ 1CED	ᳶ 1CF6	᳙ 1CD9	ॖ 0956		₹ 20B9	√ 221A

General paper on Indic scripts
https://www.w3.org/2002/Talks/09-ri-indic/indic-paper.html

Standard fonts
https://www.google.com/get/noto/

Writing
https://www.linotype.com/6896/devanagari.html

Legacy font for typing Half Letters

ट   र   ज   श   त   म   ३

http://indiatyping.com/index.php/download/201-shusha-font

Font for typing most Devanagari Vedic letters, Ligatures and Glyphs

क्र F100   च F106   भ F107   रा F10A   ꣵ F15A   ᳲ F141   F306

http://svayambhava.blogspot.in/p/siddhanta-devanagariunicode-open-type.html
https://omkarananda-ashram.org/Sanskrit/itranslator2003.htm

Pluta Vowels

In the Vedic texts, pluta vowels are encountered that are rare in classical Sanskrit. Pluta signifies elongation of a vowel while speaking, to 3 or more time lengths मात्रा । The English term for प्लुत is prolated or protacted.

Thus we have

अ Time length of one matra in speaking – short vowel ह्रस्व

आ Time length of two matras in speaking – long vowel दीर्घ

अ३ Time length of three matras in speaking – pluta vowel प्लुत

The pluta is written variously – अ३, आ३, आर — all meaning the same. A pluta vowel does not combine in sandhi.

This set has 20 letters

अ	आ	अ३
इ	ई	इ३
उ	ऊ	उ३
ऋ	ॠ	ऋ३
ऌ	-	ऌ३
ए	ऐ	ए३
ओ	औ	ओ३

E.g. for pluta vowel from a Rudrashtadhyayi text 2nd adhyaya.
एतावानस्य महिमातोज् ज्यायाँ२ श्व पूरुषः । Purushasuktam

Accented Vowels

अनुदात्त , उदात्त , स्वरित स्वराः

In the Vedic texts, accented vowels are seen. The accent signifies a change in pitch or tone of the vowel. Known as स्वर ।

अ Anudata accent to specify lowering of pitch in speaking - low

अ Udata accent to specify standard pitch in speaking - normal

अ Svarita accent to specify raising of pitch in speaking - high

Additionally, the dirgha svarita (double svarita) accent is also seen.

अ dirgha Svarita accent to specify raising of pitch for extended time length then lowering to normal – high to normal

Note - even though the texts mention उदात्त to mean raised**, in actual practise when we do Vedic chanting**, the Udata Svaras (unmarked letters in the text) are chanted in normal tone and Anudatas are clearly lowered while Svaritas are in high pitch.

अ अ अं आ आ आं अँ आँ

इ इ इं ई ई ईं इँ ईँ

उ उ उं ऊ ऊ ऊं उँ ऊँ

ऋ ऋ ऋं ॠ ॠ ॠं

ऌ ऌ ऌं

ए ए एं ऐ ऐ ऐं एँ ऐँ

ओ ओ ओं औ औ औं ओँ औँ

E.g. for accented vowel from a Rudrashtadhyayi text 2nd adhyaya.

एतावानस्य महिमातोज् ज्यायाँ २ श्र पूरुषः । Purusha Suktam

E.g. for accented vowel from a Ganapati Atharvashirsha text.

गणादिं पूर्वमुच्चार्य वर्णादीं स्तदनन्तरम् । अनुस्वारꣵ परतरः । अर्धेँन्दुलसितम् ।

Nasalized Consonants

The 5th of row class consonants are nasalized, i.e. they must be uttered with emphasis on the nose. Thus ङ् ञ् ण् न् म् are pronounced from their respective places as given and also from the nose, hence called Anunasika i.e. Nasalized.

In the Vedic texts, nasalized semivowels are also noticed. Only the three semivowel consonants viz. य् ल् व् can be nasalized in certain situations of Sandhi. These are then written with a candrabindu as यँ , लँ , वँ respectively.

This set has 8 letters

ङ्   ञ्   ण्   न्   म्

यँ   लँ   वँ

E.g. for nasalized semivowel from a Rudram text.

त्र्यम्बकयँ यजामहे सुगन्धि पुष्टिवर्धनम् ।

E.g. for nasalized semivowel from a Guru Puja text.

तत् पदं दर्शितयँ येन तस्मै श्री गुरवे नमः ।

Nasalization of Vowels

A vowel may be nasalized due to a specific Sandhi situation. Thus अ becomes अँ , आ becomes आँ , इ becomes इँ and so on.

This set has 15 letters

अँ	आँ	अँ३
इँ	ईँ	इँ३
उँ	ऊँ	उँ३
एँ	एँ	एँ३
ओँ	औँ	औँ३

Note – The eternal sound Om ओम् = nasalized ओ = ओँ = ॐ

Its enunciation would be Aum or Om or Onkara as per context or tradition.

E.g. for nasalized vowel from a Rudrashtadhyayi text 2nd adhyaya.
एतावानस्य महिमातोज् ज्यायाँ २ श्च पूरुषः । Purusha Suktam

E.g. for nasalized vowel from a Rudrashtadhyayi text 5th adhyaya.
अहींश्च सर्वाञ् जम्भयन्त्सर्वांश्च यातुधान्योऽधराचीः परासुव । Namakam / Shat-Rudriya

E.g. for nasalized vowel from a RigVeda text Mandala 1.4.13.
सुसमिद्धो न आवह देवाँ अग्ने हविष्मते ।

Use of candrabindu is common in Hindi and Marathi literature.

Alphabet table for a Vowel

Vowel अ can take the following 18 forms.

Non-nasalized निर् अनुनासिक　　　　Nasalized अनुनासिक

अ	आ	अ३	Regular	अँ	आँ	अँ३
अ	अ॒	अं	Accented Short	अँ	अँ॒	अँ
आ	आ॒	आं	Accented Long	आँ	आँ॒	आँ

Note – Regular and Accented seem to have the same forms अ , अँ repeated, however one is a Regular form and the other is an Udata accented form of Vedic Sanskrit.

Vowel अ can take the additional 2 forms of accent dirgha Svarita.

अ॑॑　　आ॑॑

Similarly Vowels इ , उ can take these 18 + 2 = 20 forms.

Vowel ऋ can take the 18 forms. Dirgha Svarita not noticed.
Vowel ऌ can take the 12 forms only as long ॡ is not noticed.

Diphthong Vowels ए , ओ have the following 12 forms.

Non-nasalized निर् अनुनासिक　　　　Nasalized अनुनासिक

ए	ऐ	ए३	Regular	एँ	ऐँ	एँ३
ए	ए॒	एं	Accented	एँ	एँ॒	एँ

Additional 2 forms of accent dirgha Svarita

ए॑॑　　एं॑॑

Maheshwar Sutras

माहेश्वराणि सूत्राणि Encompasses sounds that are the foundation of the Devanagari Alphabet. Attributed to Maharishi Panini circa 600 BC.

1	अ इ उ ण्	All vowels = अ च् letters
2	ऋ ऌ क्	Simple vowels = अ क् letters
3	ए ओ ङ्	Diphthongs = ए च् letters
4	ऐ औ च्	Semivowels = य ण् letters
Vowel – Consonant boundary		
5	ह य व र ट्	All consonants = ह ल् letters
6	ळँ ण्	=ल्+अँ, No nasal equiv for र्
7	ञ म ङ ण न म्	5th of row = Nasals = अ म् letters
8	झ भ ञ्	4th of row = झ ष् letters
9	घ ढ ध ष्	are all soft consonants
10	ज ब ग ड द् श्	3rd of row = ज श् letters (soft)
11	ख फ छ ठ थँ च ट त व्	1st and 2nd of row = ख य् letters
12	क प य्	are all hard consonants
13	श ष स र्	Sibilants (hard) = श र् letters
14	ह ळ्	Aspirate is soft

From these 14 Sutras are cognised the 44 Pratyaharas (Arrays), used in the Ashtadhyayi of Panini, and the precursor for modern day computer programming code.

Pronunciation of Sanskrit Letters

उच्चारणं

अ son आ father इ it ई beat उ full ऊ pool ऋ rhythm

ॠ marine ऌ revelry ॡ ए play ऐ aisle ओ go औ loud

अं Anusvara is pure nasal – close the lips – similar to म्

अः Visarga is Breath release like ह and preceding vowel sound

e.g. Pronounce नमः as नमह , शान्तिः as शान्तिहि , विष्णुः as विष्णुहु

क seeK	ख Khan	ग Get	घ loGHut	ङ sing
च Chunk	छ catchhim	ज Jump	झ heDGEhog	ञ bunch
ट True	ठ anTHill	ड Drum	ढ goDHead	ण under
त Tamil	थ Thunder	द That	ध breaTHE	न nut
प Put	फ Fruit	ब Bin	भ abhor	म much

य loYal र Red ल Luck व Vase श Sure ष Shun स So Hum ह

Conjuncts in general – first utter the top part and then the bottom one, e.g.

Bhagavad Gita 10.16 तिष्ठसि -> ष् ठ ,

Bhagavad Gita 10.23 शङ्करश्चास्मि -> ङ् क , श् च

Specific Conjuncts

ह् ण = ह्ण , ह् न = ह्न , ह् म = ह्म

Utter with emphasis on the chest, first the nasal and then the aspiration, e.g. Brahma = ब्रह्म *Pronounce as **Bramha***

Shiksha Vedanga – Science of Pronunciation

Sanskrit is a language that was orally passed on from generation to generation. There are many sections in the Vedic and later texts that talk about the letters of the alphabet and their proper intonation, enunciation and phonetics शिक्षा ।

Taittiriya Upanishad Shiksha Valli
शीक्षां व्याख्यास्यामः । वर्णः स्वरः । मात्रा बलम् । साम सन्तानः ।
इत्युक्तः शीक्षाध्यायः ॥ १.२ (Chapter 1 Anuvaka 2)

Taittiriya Pratisakhya तैत्तिरीय प्रातिशाख्य
अथ वर्णसमाम्नायः ॥ १॥ (Chapter 1)
स्वराः स्पर्शात् तथा अन्तःस्था ऊष्माणः च अथ दशिंताः ।
विसर्ग_अनुस्वार_ळाः च नासिक्याः पञ्च च उदिताः ॥

Paniniya Shiksha पाणिनीय शिक्षा लघु पाठः / वृद्ध पाठः
आकाशवायुप्रभवः शरीरात् समुच्चरन् वक्त्रमुपैति नादः । १.१

Paniniya Shiksha पाणिनीय शिक्षा श्लोकात्मिका
अथ शिक्षां प्रवक्ष्यामि पाणिनीयं मतं यथा । १.१

The Rigved Pratisakhya ऋग्वेद प्रातिशाख्य and Vajasneyi Pratisakhya वाजसनेयी प्रातिशाख्य are also notable texts on शिक्षा ।

Utter each letter clearly and distinctly, with proper position of the tongue in the mouth. This is the aim of the Shiksha texts. It will take some time to practise and getting used to the correct method of reading a Sanskrit letter and text. However it is most rewarding, as our anatomy, bones and muscles are all connected to sound, the key aspect of the fundamental element space.

Place & Effort of Enunciation

Place of speech	Vowels स्वर		Row Consonants व्यञ्जन					Semi vowel	Sibilant
			Alpaprana		Mahaprana				
	Short	Long	1st	2nd	3rd	4th	5th		
कण्ठ	अ	आ	क	ख	ग	घ	ङ		
तालु	इ	ई	च	छ	ज	झ	ञ	य	श
मूर्धा	ऋ	ॠ	ट	ठ	ड	ढ	ण	र	ष
दन्त	ऌ		त	थ	द	ध	न	ल	स
ओष्ठ	उ	ऊ	प	फ	ब	भ	म		
Consonants are supplied with vowel अ to aid enunciation									

कण्ठ – तालु	ए ऐ	Diphthongs have twin places of utterance, being compound vowels
कण्ठ – ओष्ठ	ओ औ	
दन्त – ओष्ठ	व	The vakara is different from the other semivowels as it has twin places of utterance
नासिक्य	ः , अं	Anusvara is a pure Nasal
अनुनासिका	ः , ॐ , यँ	Candrabindu means Nasalization

कण्ठ Soft, Mahaprana	ह	Hakara is an Aspirate. It is sounded like a soft release of breath
	◌ः	Visarga is an Aspirate. It is sounded like ह alongwith its preceding vowel
Ardha Visarga ◌ः is also written as ✕		
Base of tongue Hard, Alpaprana	◌ः or ✕	Jihvamuliya pronounce as ह् (a visarga preceding क , ख)
ओष्ठ Hard, Alpaprana or ꣳ	◌ः or ✕	Upadhmaniya pronounce as फ़् (a visarga preceding प , फ)

कण्ठ्य Guttural or Velar	तालव्य Palatal	मूर्धन्य Cerebral or Retroflex or Lingual	दन्त्य Dental	ओष्ठ्य Labial

All vowels and semi vowels are termed voiced घोष वर्ण । This means that a background sound is produced from the tremor in the vocal cords in addition to the active sound produced in speaking. The 3rd, 4th and 5th letters of the row class consonants are also घोष वर्ण ।

The 1st and 2nd letters of the row class consonants, the sibilants and the aspirate are termed अघोष वर्ण । This means that no background sound arises from the tremor in the vocal cords.

All row consonants are termed स्पर्श वर्ण Tongue makes contact

http://rachelsenglish.com/ending-voiced-vs-unvoiced-consonants/

The unit of time for enunication is a short vowel, having 1 matra.
The long vowels and diphthongs have 2 matras.
A consonant has only ½ matra and it is supplied with a vowel for proper enunciation.

VOWELS स्वर
> Long Vowels are sounded twice as long as the short vowels.
> DIPHTHONGS सन्ध्यक्षर (सन्धि – अक्षर) Are combinations of two vowels and are sounded long.

GUTTURALS कण्ठ्य (also known as VELAR)
> Sounded from the throat with the tongue resting.

PALATALS तालव्य
> Sounded with the tongue raised slightly.

CEREBRALS मूर्धन्य (also known as RETROFLEX or LINGUAL)
> Sounded with the tongue touching the roof of the mouth.

DENTALS दन्त्य
> Sounded with the tongue distinctly touching the teeth.

LABIALS ओष्ठ्य
> Sounded with the lips distinctly touching each other.

Letter Names

The question arises if there are names for letters? Yes, there are. A common practice is to attach कार to a letter and that becomes its name.

The vowel अ is called अकार
The vowel आ is called आकार
The vowel इ is called इकार , etc.

The consonant क is called ककार
The consonant ख is called खकार
The consonant ग is called गकार , etc.

There is also a name for all vowels put together. It is अच्
There is also a name for all consonants put together. It is हल्

Then there is the name वर्ग for the 25 row class consonants.
The first row beginning with क् and comprising of the letters क् ख् ग् घ् ङ् is named कवर्ग or simply कु(कुँ=क् उँ, where उँ is a discardable tag)
The second row beginning with च् and comprising of the letters च् छ् ज् झ् is named चवर्ग or simply चु (चुँ) ।
The third row beginning with ट् and comprising of the letters ट् ठ् ड् ढ् ण् is named टवर्ग or simply टु (टुँ) ।
The fourth row beginning with त् and comprising of the letters त् थ् द् ध् न् is named तवर्ग or simply तु (तुँ) ।
The fifth row beginning with प् and comprising of the letters प् फ् ब् भ् म् is named पवर्ग or simply पु (पुँ) ।

There is a special name for र् । It is commonly called the Repha.

Ayogavaha

The Ayogavāha class of characters do not exist independently, but are born in the case of specific combinations of letters in a sentence. Ayogavāha sounds are Candrabindu, Anusvāra, Visarga, Ardha Visarga (Jihvāmūlīya and Upadhmānīya), Nāsikya, Yama and Svarabhakti. These cannot be pronounced independently but depend on a vowel, e.g. अ to be enunciated. Hence named अ–योग–वाह A-yoga-vaha = in flowing union with "A".

CANDRABINDU ँ and ANUSVĀRA ं

Sounds can be produced from the mouth, from the mouth with emphasis on the nose anunāsika, and from the nose alone with the mouth shut. *The term* **nasalization** *is employed to denote that emphasis is on the nose, whereas* **nasal** *means use of nose alone.*

Candrabindu indicates that a vowel is to be pronounced as nasalized. It can also indicate the nasalization of the consonants य् , ल् and व् I Thus the mouth and nose both are employed in sounding the chandrabindu.

Anusvāra is a character that denotes the pure nasal. Thus, it is slightly different than the म् which is an anunāsika. Technically it should be pronounced with the mouth shut. It is doable for those who learnt it in their childhood. Most of us pronounce it like the म् in which the lips touch and then open. The anusvāra represents the nasal of the type of letter it precedes; e.g. गंगा = गङ्गा = *gaṅga (river Ganges)*. Refer Ashtadhyayi of Panini 8.3.4 अनुनासिकात् परोऽनुस्वारः appearance of anusvara.

VISARGA ः

Pronounced like *huh* with a soft release of breath. During reading, the visarga takes on the addition of its preceding vowel. Thus utter रामः as ramaha, हरिः as harihi, विष्णुः as vishnuhu.

ARDHA VISARGA ᵡ (Vedic texts only) JIHVAMULIYA, UPADHMANIYA

The visarga becomes an ardha visarga in specific sandhi situations. If it is facing a क or ख , the visarga is called an ardha visarga named Jihvāmūlīya and is written as ᵡ or **X**. If it is facing a प or फ , the visarga is called an ardha visarga named Upadhmānīya and is written as ᵡ or ꣵ. In some earlier texts ꣵ denotes upadhmaniya.

NĀSIKYA हुँ (Vedic texts only) नासिक्य

This nasikya sound is popular in Art of Living programs, however the grammatical connotation is different.

YAMA ꣺ ꣸ (sounded like गुँ , गंꣿ Vedic texts only) कꣿ ँ खुँ गुँ घुँ - यम

Means addition of a consonant between a consonant and a nasal during Vedic chanting. कꣿ ँ is an abbreviation for the initial row consonant letters of each of the five rows viz. क् च् ट् त् प् । कꣿ ँ = क् ुँ where ुँ is a meta tag letter. Characters ꣺ ꣸ represent

accentuated anusvāra preceding र , श ष स , ह । The ꣺ supposedly follows short vowels, and ꣸ follows long vowels in the Rudra Puja chanting of the South Indian Krishna Yajur Veda tradition. Some grammarians are of the viewpoint that the yama sound ꣸ indicates the nasalization in particular sandhi cases when the following letter is a sibilant or a repha. In the Rudrashtadhyayi chanting followed in the North Indian tradition, the ज gets accented as य (termed heavy य) in some cases, while ष and gets enunciated as ख ।

SVARABHAKTI (anaptyxis) र॒ , ल॒ (स्वर भक्ति)

Means addition of a vowel between two consonants to aid enunciation. A vowel sound akin to ऋ ऌ inserted between र or ल and a following consonant. This sound is supposed to last for a quarter matra मात्रा called अणु । Sound that is half time period of अणु is termed परमाणु ।

Letters that Look similar

क	ख	ग	घ	ङ
11	12	13	14	15
च	छ	ज	झ	अ
21	22	23	24	25
ट	ठ	ड	ढ	ण
31	32	33	34	35
त	थ	द	ध	न
41	42	43	44	45
प	फ	ब	भ	म
51	52	53	54	55
य र ल व		श ष स ह		

12 ख रव (र adjacent to व in a word)

14 घ ध 44

15 ङ ड 33

23 ज अ 25

34 ढ द 43

54 भ म 55

Letters that Sound similar

क 11	ख 12	ग 13	घ 14	ङ 15
च 21	छ 22	ज 23	झ 24	ञ 25
ट 31	ठ 32	ड 33	ढ 34	ण 35
त 41	थ 42	द 43	ध 44	न 45
प 51	फ 52	ब 53	भ 54	म 55
य र ल व		श ष स ह		

15 ङ अ 25

35 ण न 45

33 ड ढ 34

श ष

Conjuncts

Famous conjuncts क्ष , ज्ञ , श्र

क्ष = क् ष , ज्ञ = ज् ञ , श्र = श् र

Common conjuncts त्र , त्त , क्त , द्य , ह्म ,

त्र = त् र , त्त = त् त , क्त = क् त , द्य = द् य , ह्म = ह् म

Repha conjuncts
A preceding repha goes on the top like a hook.

र्क = र् क , र्प = र् प

A following repha is written like a forward slanting slash.

क्र = क् र , प्र = प् र

However, in these conjuncts a following repha is like a circumflex.

ट्र = ट् र , ठ्र, ड्र, ढ्र, छ्र, ल्र

Punctuation marks

Sanskrit text whether prose or poetry has a minimum of punctuations. The only visible ones are

AVAGRAHA ऽ

>Marks the elision of initial अ due to sandhi.

Double AVAGRAHA ऽऽ

>Marks the elision of initial आ due to sandhi.

DANDA also known as VIRAMA

>। marks the end of a sentence.

>॥ marks the end of a paragraph.

>In the case of poetry, a single virama signifies a pause in reading or a half-verse. A double virama means a complete verse.

Abbreviation ॰

>A small circle signifies a shortened word or verse.

Some other punctuations are in the form of regular letters.

च means the conjunction "and"

>which is also commonly employed as a comma. So we may write *Time, Space, Air, Water and Matter* in Sanskrit as काल खम् वायु जलम् वस्तु च ।

इति means the preposition "thus"

>which is also commonly employed as quotation marks. *He said "Shiva is Beautiful"* = शिवम् सुन्दरं इति सः उवाच ।

किम् means the question "what"

>which is also commonly employed as a question mark. *What is your name?* is written as भवतः नाम किम् ।

हे means hailing someone "hey"

>which is also commonly employed as an exclamation! *Hey Ram!* is written as हे राम ।

Vowel Matras

A vowel follows a consonant and gets joined to it. A consonant without a vowel will have the presence of halant ् e.g. क् । Whereas letters having a vowel will not have the halant e.g. क ।

अ when joined to क् becomes क and so on.

आ when joined to क् becomes का and so on. ा

इ when joined to क् becomes कि and so on. ि

ई when joined to क् becomes की and so on. ी

उ when joined to क् becomes कु and so on. ु

ऊ when joined to क् becomes कू and so on. ू

ऋ when joined to क् becomes कृ and so on. ृ

ॠ when joined to क् becomes कॄ and so on. ॄ

ऌ when joined to क् becomes कॢ and so on. ॢ

ए when joined to क् becomes के and so on. े

ऐ when joined to क् becomes कै and so on. ै

ओ when joined to क् becomes को and so on. ो

औ when joined to क् becomes कौ and so on. ौ

Anusvara ं joins to a vowel to give अं , कं , किं , कुं etc.

Visarga : joins to a vowel to give अः , कः , किः , कुः etc.

र् Repha with उ , ऊ is different because it goes in the middle रु , रू

Writing Matras

Vowel matras मात्रा are written after the letter, above the letter, or below the letter.

ाT in all cases and the special case of र ्उ and र ्ऊ
After the letter e.g. आ , रु , रू

कि ी , े ै , ो ौ
Above the letter e.g. कि , खी , गे , सै , चो , जौ ,

ु ू , ृ ॄ , ॢ
Below the letter e.g. पु , फू , वृ , कृ , कृ ,

Some more markings

्
To specify a half-letter the halant is added below e.g. ट् , ड् , य् , ब्

ँ ं
To specify Nasalization, Candrabindu or Anusvara is added above e.g. माँ , नं

ः
To specify aspiration, Visarga is added after e.g. मः , तिः , नुः

Similarly for conjuncts
ध्मा, च्छे , न्यू , न्तिः , क्रू

Alphabet table for letter "ka" क

Sanskrit alphabet written using the letter क

Mātrās

क का कि की कु कू के कै को कौ कं कः

कृ कॄ कॢ

Accents

क क॒ क॑ क᳚   का का॒ का॑ का᳚   कि कि॒ कि॑ कि᳚   की की॒ की॑ की᳚

कु कु॒ कु॑ कु᳚   कू कू॒ कू॑ कू᳚   के के॒ के॑ के᳚   कै कै॒ कै॑ कै᳚

को को॒ को॑ को᳚   कौ कौ॒ कौ॑ कौ᳚

Nasalization

कँ काँ किँ कीँ कुँ कूँ केँ कैँ कोँ कौँ

Pluta

क३ का३ कि३ की३ कु३ कू३ के३ कै३ को३ कौ३

Ayogavahas occur on specific combinations of letters

मामक⋆पाण्डवाश्चैव   त्र्यम्बकयँयजामहे   हिँसीः   अहीँश्च   द्विपदा᳴यश्

Vedic and Classical Sanskrit

वैदिक तथा लौकिक संस्कृत

Vedic texts such as the Taittiriya Upanishad Shiksha Valli, the Paniniya Shiksha and the Taittiriya Pratisakhya give detailed enumeration of sounds and letters in grammar.

All of these sounds and letters got mingled and reused in various languages around the globe as man journeyed, explored and met peoples from various lands. Some of the vedic sounds are still used in languages such as English, French, Spanish, Tamil, Greek, Latin, Hittite, Russian, Hebrew, Chinese, Japanese, Arabic, Urdu, German, Hindi, Marathi, Nepali while classical Sanskrit has retired them.

Conversely, these languages have had an influence on Sanskrit so its forms in Hindi, Marathi, Nepali have some extra characters that seem to be absent in classical Sanskrit.

Letters ळ and ळ्ह

अग्निमीळे पुरोहितं यज्ञस्य देवमृत्विजम् । Rigveda 1.1.1.1

अग्ने मृळीकं वरुणे सचा विदो मरुत्सु विश्वभानुषु । Rigveda 4.1.1.3

दृळ्हं नरो वचसा दैव्येन व्रजं गोमन्तमुशिजो वि वव्रुः । Rigveda 4.1.1.15

This letter ळ is frequent in Marathi but rare in Hindi. Present day
Sanskrit does not use it.

Accents Udata, Anudata _   , Svarita ' , Dirgha Svarita "

Ayogavaha Sounds ArdhaVisarga, Yama, Nasikya, Svarabhakti
    In the chanting of Rudrashtadhyayi North Indian tradition
    the sound य (a palatal) is pronounced as ज (a palatal) in
    particular instances. Written in the text as य ।

    Also in some sandhi situations the sound ष (a retroflex) is
    uttered as ख (a guttural). This is seen in the Shukla Yajurved
    Madhyandini Samhita. (Rudrashtadhyayi chanting North
    Indian tradition). Here when ष is followed by a consonant it
    is uttered as ख , except when ष is followed by the retroflex
    consonants ट ठ ड ढ ण then it is uttered as ष ।

Nukta
    The nukta is a dot placed below-left of a letter. It finds use in
    Hindi for special enunciation of some words and is also due
    to the influence of Arabic and Urdu.
    क़ ख़ ग़ ज़ ड़ ढ़ फ़ य़
    Nukta is not seen in Sanskrit.

Anusvara and Candrabindu usage varies in each language that use
the Devanagari script.

Vedic Accents

स्वरः Udata, Anudata, Svarita, Dirgha Svarita

Accents are marks on the vowels that change the pitch.
Accents are used to highlight that a particular vowel is to be pronounced in a different pitch. Vary the frequency, vary the tone so that the chanting is noticed by the listener appropriately.
These are given in the text by various marks under or on the vowel.

A syllable may be pronounced
from the belly, Anudāta, by dropping the neck slightly = low pitch
from the heart, Udāta, by keeping a straight face = normal pitch
from the forehead, Svarita, by raising the neck slightly = high pitch
elongating the time of enunciation, dīrgha Svarita = high to normal

अनुदात्त Anudāta, underline for a vowel, signifies that the pitch is to be lowered, i.e. the sound should come from the belly.

अन् + उदात्तः = अनुदात्तः = ◌̲

उदात्त Udāta – The normal chant, keeping a straight face. There is no marking for उदात्तः l When Anudāta is followed by Udāta, or vice versa, then a change in pitch will be noticeable.

Svarita – Raise in pitch by lifting the head slightly.
स्वरितः = ◌̍ a vertical bar on the vowel

Dīrgha Svarita – raising the pitch for a longer duration

दीर्घ स्वरितः =   two vertical bars on the vowel – During chanting, it is noticeable by pronouncing the vowel, giving a short gap, then again pronouncing the vowel.

Listen to vedic chants to notice how the change in pitch works.
https://www.youtube.com/watch?v=vQjBQJqi0Ak Rudram Challakere Brothers
https://www.youtube.com/watch?v=clb22c3QiGc Havan with Rudrashtadhyayi - Vedic fire ritual

Early Scripts and Languages

The Brahmi, Nagari, Gupta, Sharada scripts were used to write the Pali, Prakrit, Magadhi and Sanskrit languages that flourished in India and South East Asia.

Early inscriptions in the Brahmi script date from the times of Emperor Ashoka circa 250 BC.

The Grantha is a historical script that was used to write Sanskrit in Tamil Nadu. Its use gradually declined over the last century and gave way to Devanagari for Sanskrit texts.

https://en.wikipedia.org/wiki/Brahmi_script Brahmi wikipedia
http://www.virtualvinodh.com/ Vinodh Rajan's blog on scripts

Languages that use Devanagari Script

Devanagari is a descendant of the Brahmi script that was used in India a thousand years ago. Currently over a hundred languages use the Devanagari script. Some of these languages are

- Assamese or Bodo
- Hindi
- Konkani
- Marathi
- Nepali

The Devanagari script is known as *abugida*. Abugida means a form of writing in which the vowels get joined to consonants in a syllable and are treated as a single unit. Such writing is typical of scripts from South Asia.

A Complete Character Set

For typing in Devanagari to be versatile, the following characters need to be present at the minimum in a font set.

Standard set

Standard set with ability to type half-forms of letters e.g. र् ग् च्

Standard set with ability to type conjuncts e.g. ज्ह ह्ल ह्व ह्ल न्स्म ङ्क

Standard set with ability to type standalone characters
>	Candrabindu, Anusvara, Visarga, Virama for special use

Extended Vedic set
>	for accents and ayogavaha sounds and nasalization

>	for enunciating य in specific cases = य़

>	for characters ळ , ऴ्ह

Hindi-Marathi-Nepali-Bihari-Kashmiri set
>	for nukta as in Hindi ज़, letter ळ for Marathi, etc.

Backward compatibility set
>	for letters that have changed shape over time in texts

>	e.g. अ to अ, झ to झ, क्ष for क्ष , ण to ण , त्र to त्र

Punctuation set for virama, danda, etc.

Special characters set - for rupee symbol ₹ , square root √ for
>	displaying the dhatus, etc.

Roman transliteration set – English letters with diacritical marks
>	e.g. iso 15919 letters ñ ṅ ṇ

Correct spacing, height, width for matras and accents and diacrics

The Unicode Standard 9.0 allots the range
>	0900 – 097F for Devanagari
>	A8E0 – A8FF for Devanagari extended
>	1CD0 – 1CFF for Vedic Extensions

http://www.unicode.org/charts/
http://software.sil.org/gentium/support/character-set-support/

Standard set

अ आ इ ई उ ऊ ऋ ॠ ऌ ॡ   ए ऐ ओ औ   अं अः

क	ख	ग	घ	ङ
च	छ	ज	झ	ञ
ट	ठ	ड	ढ	ण
त	थ	द	ध	न
प	फ	ब	भ	म

य र ल व

श ष स   ह

० १ २ ३ ४ ५ ६ ७ ८ ९

Standard set with Half-forms of consonants

क क्	ख ख्	ग ग्	घ घ्	ङ
च च्	छ छ्	ज ज्	झ झ्	ञ ञ्
ट	ठ	ड	ढ	ण ण्
त त्	थ थ्	द	ध ध्	न न्
प प्	फ फ्	ब ब्	भ भ्	म म्
य य् र लल् व व्				
श श् ष ष् स स् ह ह्				

Matras, nukta, nasalization, accents, diacritics

For beautiful typesetting, the following characters should be properly spaced in a Devanagari font.

The vedic accent anudata below a vowel

e.g. कु̱ rather than कु or कु

The vedic accent svarita above a vowel

e.g. की॑ rather than की

The vedic accent double svarita above a vowel

e.g. की॑॑ rather than की

Written versus Spoken

Sanskrit words in a sentence coalesce due to conjuncts, sandhis or compounding. Hence written Sanskrit is ***slightly different*** than spoken Sanskrit. As such a teacher is required for one to learn how to read the scriptures or vedic texts, especially the Bhagavad Gita and the Rudra Puja.

https://www.zorbabooks.com/store/religion/bhagavad-gita-for-chanting/ Bhagavad Gita for Chanting

https://www.zorbabooks.com/store/religion/rudra-puja/ Rudra Puja

https://www.amazon.com/dp/B0718W5ZQF Bhagavad Gita Reader - All verses in 4 quarters

Avagraha Ayogavaha Visarga Anusvara

Reading or chanting a Sanskrit text takes into account the appearance of Ayogavaha characters. These characters are uttered in a specific way, that is usually taught in a gurukul system.

Even though traditionally the ayogavaha characters are only specified in the Vedic texts, by definition we can include them to mean the Visarga and the Anusvara.

अवग्रह Avagraha ऽ is not to be chanted, i.e. it is a silent letter.

> It signifies that an अ has been dropped due to sandhi.

> e.g. Recite प्रथमोऽध्यायः as प्रथमोध्यायः ,

> verse 2.14 आगमापयिनोऽनित्याः as आगमापयिनोनित्याः , etc.

विसर्ग Visarga ◌ः is pronounced variously, a brief mention

> A visarga is pronounced aspirated ह् followed by the sound

> of the preceding vowel. Thus नमः is to be chanted as नम ह

> verse 2.41 बुद्धिः is to be chanted as बुद्धि हि

> verse 2.43 स्वर्गपराः is to be chanted as स्वर्गपरा हा

> verse 2.47 कर्मफलहेतुर्भूः is to be chanted as कर्मफलहेतुर्भू हू

> This rule is valid only when a visarga is at the end, i.e. a virama is present. This rule also applies when a visarga is followed by a pause, as at a quarter verse.

However, a visarga in close proximity with another letter gets replaced with another letter or even gets dropped. This is reflected in this book by substituting the changed letter. (popular editions of the Gita show the visarga rather than the actual letter that is to be chanted). E.g.

Visarga when followed by श or च is pronounced as श्

तेजः क्षमा धृतिः शौचम् ,   अद्रोहो नातिमानिता । तेजश् क्षमा धृतिश् शौचम्

भवन्ति सम्पदं दैवीम् ,   अभिजातस्य भारत ॥ १६.३

Visarga when followed by स or त is pronounced as स्

कार्यकरणकर्तृत्वे ,   हेतुः प्रकृतिरुच्यते ।

पुरुषः सुखदुःखानाम् , भोक्तृत्वे हेतुरुच्यते ॥ १३.२० (पुरुषस् सुखदुःखानाम्)

Visarga when followed by vowel or soft consonant is dropped or changes to ओ as per context. Consider verse 2.16 नासतः विद्यते भावः नाभावः विद्यते सतः । and as it appears in popular editions नासतो विद्यते भावो नाभावो विद्यते सतः । because the visarga has been changed to ओ due to sandhi. And here in this book, due to the pause in chanting नासतो विद्यते भावः ,   नाभावो विद्यते सतः । the visarga is shown because भावो is to be chanted as भावः i.e. as भावह् ।

Similarly

पिताहमस्य जगतः ,   माता धाता पितामहः ।

वेद्यं पवित्रमोङ्कारः ,   ऋक्साम यजुरेव च ॥ ९.१७

येऽप्यन्यदेवता भक्ताः ,   यजन्ते श्रद्धयान्विताः ।

तेऽपि मामेव कौन्तेय ,   यजन्त्यविधिपूर्वकम् ॥ ९.२३

Also, a visarga changes to a repha in certain instances, or gets dropped in other cases.

Ardha Visarga ⨯ जिह्वामूलीय / उपधमानीय

Optionally, a visarga ◌ः becomes an ardha visarga when the following letter is a क or ख and is called jihvamuliya. When the following letter is प or फ it is called upadhmaniya. But it remains a visarga when the following letter is क्ष (क्‌ष). Visarga preceding क, ख is pronounced aspirated ह्

बुद्धियुक्तो जहातीह ,   उभे सुकृतदुष्कृते ।

तस्माद् योगाय युज्यस्व , 	योगꣳ कर्मसु कौशलम् ॥ २.५०

Visarga preceding प, फ is pronounced aspirated फ़

धर्मक्षेत्रे कुरुक्षेत्रे , 	समवेता युयुत्सवः ।

मामकाꣳ पाण्डवाश्चैव , 	किम् अकुर्वत सञ्जय ॥ १.१

Notice that generally a visarga is at the end of a word, but in rare cases it comes within a word (verse 13.20 सुखदुःखानाम् , verse 18.3 यज्ञदानतपꣳकर्म).

Anusvara ं is pronounced as nasalized म् ।

However Sandhi grammar rules state that Anusvara changes to a corresponding nasal when followed by a class consonant, *albeit optionally*. Very few pandits make the Anusvara sound as ङ् when followed by ग, as ञ् when followed by च or as न् when followed by त / द ।

पश्यैतां पाण्डुपुत्राणाम् , 	आचार्य महतीं चमूम् । (महतीञ् चमूम्)

व्यूढां द्रुपदपुत्रेण , 	तव शिष्येण धीमता ॥ १.३ (व्यूढान् द्रुपदपुत्रेण)

Others chant an Anusvara as यँ when followed by य ।

कर्म ब्रह्मोद्भवं विद्धि , 	ब्रह्माक्षरसमुद्भवम् ।

तस्मात् सर्वगतं ब्रह्म , 	नित्यं यज्ञे प्रतिष्ठितम् ॥ ३.१५ नित्यँ यज्ञे

In any case it is ok if Anusvara is pronounced as म् ।

Specific Conjuncts

ह्न , ह्ण , ह्म These conjuncts are chanted as नः , णः , मः resp.

पवनꣳ पवतामस्मि , 	रामः शस्त्रभृतामहम् ।

झषाणां मकरश्चास्मि , 	स्रोतसामस्मि जाह्नवी ॥ १०.३१ जानःवी

i.e. though it is ह् न , pronunciation is न ह । These letters are chanted with emphasis on the chest.

स्फोटन Sphotana

When a व्यञ्जन is followed by a क or क्ष there is a natural pause in reading aloud.

Modern Editors

How to type in Sanskrit?

A standard method to insert any symbol is to look up its code in the Unicode Chart. Then type that code and press **ALT+X** keys.
e.g. to insert the rupee symbol, type its code 20B9. Pressing **ALT+X** keys converts it to ₹ i.e. type 20B9**ALT+X**
e.g. to type the Om symbol, type its code 0950. Pressing **ALT+X** keys converts it to ॐ i.e. type 0950**ALT+X**

Unicode charts are available at http://www.unicode.org/charts/

However, this method will prove cumbersome to type a page or continuous text in Sanskrit. So the proper way is to ***enable the Sanskrit or Hindi keyboard*** in Windows or Mac or the smartphone.

OpenOffice, MS Word, Adobe Pagemaker and Indesign, and Tex are the standard word processors.
https://www.openoffice.org/
https://products.office.com/en-in/word
http://www.adobe.com/in/products/indesign.html
https://www.tug.org/
https://www.ctan.org/tex-archive/language/devanagari/velthuis/?lang=en

Additional writers with support for typing in Indian languages are
http://software.nhm.in/products/writer
http://www.lipikaar.com/
http://www.lexilogos.com/keyboard/sanskrit_devanagari.htm
http://www.baraha.com/

Fonts

Some good unicode compliant Devanagari fonts are
Sanskrit 2003
https://omkarananda-ashram.org/Sanskrit/itranslator2003.htm

Siddhanta
http://svayambhava.blogspot.in/

Annapurna SIL
http://software.sil.org/annapurna/

from CDAC
https://cdac.in/index.aspx?id=dl_mlingual_tools

And some excellent legacy Devanagari fonts are
New Delhi, Kruti Dev, Chanakya, Shusha

Keyboard Mapping for Phonetic Typing

http://www.mywhatever.com/sanskrit/vidyut/index.html

https://ubcsanskrit.ca/keyboards.html

Processing Tools
http://sanskritdocuments.org/processing_tools/processing_tools.html

Devanagari Typesetting

Basic Requirements and a typical method

1. a software like MS **Word** or LaTex
2. preferably a unicode compliant font like **Sanskrit** 2003
3. print to pdf printer like **pdfCreator**
   http://www.pdfforge.org/pdfcreator
4. Enabling the **Sanskrit keyboard** in control panel - Regional & Language settings
5. After the document has been typed in Devanagari, one must print it to pdfCreator with the save setting **pdf/X**. This **embeds** all the fonts and the resulting pdf file can be easily rendered correctly on any machine, operating system, or device.

Transliteration Standards

Sanskrit words are written using Devanagari script. An English-speaking person who is used to Roman script can use the transcribing facility to read Sanskrit. There are different conventions to transcribe Devanagari to Roman script.

1. IAST
2. Hunterian system
3. National Library at Kolkata romanization
4. ISO 15919
5. Harvard-Kyoto
6. ITRANS scheme
7. Velthuis
8. SLP1

https://en.wikipedia.org/wiki/Devanagari_transliteration

Devanagari Transliteration Tool
https://www.ashtangayoga.info/sanskrit/

The ISO 15919 standard
http://www.iso.org/iso/iso_catalogue/catalogue_tc/catalogue_detail.htm?csnumber=28333

Devanagari Latin ISO 15919 Chart

a	ā	i	ī	u	ū	r̥	r̥̄	l̥	
अ	आ	इ	ई	उ	ऊ	ऋ	ॠ	ऌ	
						ॢ	ॣ	ॢ	
ē	ai	ō	au	ṁ	m̐	ḥ	Ardha visarga		
ए	ऐ	ओ	औ	ं	ँ	ः	ꣳ		
Consonants are shown with a vowel a=अ for uttering									
ka	क	ca	च	ṭa	ट	ta	त	pa	प
kha	ख	cha	छ	ṭha	ठ	tha	थ	pha	फ
ga	ग	ja	ज	ḍa	ड	da	द	ba	ब
gha	घ	jha	झ	ḍha	ढ	dha	ध	bha	भ
ṅa	ङ	ña	ञ	ṇa	ण	na	न	ma	म
ya	ra	la	va		ḷa	'			
य	र	ल	व		ळ	ऽ			
				Consonant only					
śa	ṣa	sa	ha		ka	कअ = क			
श	ष	स	ह		k	क्			

Note – halant ् is not a separate character in the transliteration.

It simply means lack of vowel in the consonant.

e.g. Both these words end in "n" but one has a halant in Devanagari. So the word without the halant has a vowel added to it in transliteration. E.g. Both these words end in "n" but one has a halant in Devanagari. So the word without the halant has a vowel added to it in transliteration.

Arjuna अर्जुन śrī bhagavān श्री भगवान्

Sanskrit Schools

Samskrita Bharati is a premier organisation that teaches Sanskrit.

http://www.vasmp.org/ Veda Agama Samskrutha Maha Pathshala
http://www.sanskrit.nic.in/ Rashtriya Sanskrit Sansthan
https://www.samskritabharati.in/ Samskrita Bharati
http://avg-sanskrit.org/ Arsha Vijnana Gurukulam
https://www.madrassanskritcollege.edu.in/
Madras Sanskrit College

https://www.chinfo.org/index.php/easy-sanskrit-course
Chinmaya Mission

http://www.rkmath.org/courses-and-syllabuses-sanskrit.aspx?pid=237
Ramakrishan Math

https://www.youtube.com/watch?v=KnIBwHJPWuA
Sanskrit Language teaching through Video
https://www.youtube.com/watch?v=9EiyBDWITcA
Spoken Sanskrit Series

http://www.columbia.edu/cu/mesaas/languages/sanskrit/
Columbia University, New York
https://www.brown.edu/academics/classics/sanskrit-studies-brown
Brown University, Rhode Island

http://www.sai.uni-heidelberg.de/abt/IND/en/links/links.php?sanskrit_studies
University of Heidelberg, Germany
https://www.bun.kyoto-u.ac.jp/en/ Kyoto University, Japan
http://www.americansanskrit.com/ American Sanskrit Institute
https://sas.fas.harvard.edu/sanskrit Harvard University
http://web.mit.edu/samskritam/www/ MIT Students

Sanskrit Book Publishers

Motilal Banarsidass, Gita Press and Samskrita Bharati are popular.

https://www.samskritabharati.in/bookstore
https://www.mlbd.com/
http://www.gitapress.org/
http://www.chowkhambasanskritseries.com/
http://chaukhambabooks.in/index.php
http://www.rkmkhar.org/ideas/bookshop/
https://www.giri.in/giri-books
http://vedah.com/
http://www.mrmlonline.com/
http://www.parimalpublication.com/

Vedanta Book House in Chamrajpet, Bangalore has a good collection of Sanskrit books from various publishers.

Sanskrit Scholars

Mataji Swamini Brahmaprakasananda Saraswati, Nagpur
http://www.arshavijnanagurukulamnagpur.org/

Pushpa Dikshit, Bilaspur
http://www.pushpadikshit.com/

A.S Sundara Murthy Sivam, Bangalore
http://www.vasmp.org/

Janardana Hegde, Bangalore
https://samskritabharati.in/

George Cardona, USA
https://www.ling.upenn.edu/people/cardona

Madhav M. Deshpande, USA
https://lsa.umich.edu/asian/people/faculty/mmdesh.html

Saroja Bhate, Pune
http://www.unipune.ac.in/dept/fine_arts/sanskrit_and_pakrit/sanpak_w
ebfiles/profile.htm

Ulrich Stiehl, Germany
http://www.sanskritweb.net/

Gary Tubb, USA
http://salc.uchicago.edu/faculty/tubb

A Sanskrit Speaking Town

Mattur in Shimoga district of Karnataka is a hamlet famous for the fact that the avaerage resident speaks Sanskrit. Its twin town Hosahalli does too.

Some other places are Ganoda hamlet in Banswara district of Rajasthan, Jhiri in Rajgarh district of Madhya Pradesh, Mohad in Narsinhpur district of Madhya Pradesh, Shyamsundarpur in Kendujhar district of Orissa, Bhantoli in Rudraprayag district of Uttarakhand.

https://en.wikipedia.org/wiki/Mattur

https://www.youtube.com/watch?v=s0I8h5oCbrQ

http://thelandoutthere.com/the-last-existing-sanskrit-village-mathur-karnataka/

http://globalvarnasramamission.blogspot.in/2012/01/five-indian-villages-where-sanskrit-is.html

https://thammayya.wordpress.com/2008/10/13/sanskrit-speaking-village-in-madhya-pradesh/

https://www.youtube.com/watch?v=lHLIy-WHDew

Complete Alphabet with Vedic Extensions

Here we list the Alphabet with all its letters, signs and symbols, as seen in Sanskrit literature, in the Devanagari script.

Om and Special Symbols

ॐ	्◌	ऽ	◌ं	◌ः
Om	halant	Avagraha	Anusvara	Visarga
U0950	U094D	U093D	U0902	U0903
◌ँ	◌़	◌ँ		
candrabindu	nukta	candra bindu rare		
U0901	U093C	U0900		

Punctuation Marks

।	॥	०	ॐ	ꣳ
Virama. Full stop. Sentence end	Purna Virama. Full Stop. Paragraph or Verse end	Abbreviation sign	Nih-Shvasa. Pause for breath intake	Flower sign. To show footnote or reference
U0964	U0965	U0970	U1CD3	

Vowel Matra Symbols

ा	ि	ी	ु	ू
आ matra	इ matra	ई matra	उ matra	ऊ matra
U093E	U093F	U0940	U0941	U0942
ृ	ॄ	ॢ	े	ै
ऋ matra	ॠ matra	ऌ matra	ए matra	ऐ matra
U0943	U0944	U0962	U0947	U0948
ो	ौ			
ओ matra	औ matra			
U094B	U094C			

Symbols used in print or teaching but unused in literature

ॡ	ॣ			
vowel	ॡ matra			
U0961	U0963			

Ayogavaha Symbols due to Sandhi

◌ं अं	◌ँ अँ	◌ँ अँ	Vowel Nasalization
U0905+0902	U0905+0901	U0905+0900	
यँ	लँ	वँ	Semivowel Nasalization
U092F+0901+1CED	U0932+0901+1CED	U0935+0901+1CED	
◌ः अः	Aspiration	◌ꣳ अꣳ	Ardha Visarga – jihvamuliya or upadhmaniya
U0905+0903		U0905+1CF2	

Accent Svara marks for change in pitch while chanting

◌॒	◌॑	◌᳚	Vowel Accent Mark
U0952	U0951	U1CDA	
अ॒	अ॑	अ᳚	As seen in print in presence of Vowel
Anudatta	Svarita	Dirgha Svarita	Accent Name
Low pitch	High to normal pitch	High to low pitch for longer duration	meaning

Anusvara Independent Symbols due to Sandhi

Anusvara written independently when facing a sibilant or a repha, a long anusvara by Sandhi.

꣙	꣚	꣛	꣜	
U1CE9 + 0902	U1CEA + 0902	U1CEB + 0902	U1CEC + 0902	

Above symbols are also seen with Candrabindu. ꣚ U1CEA+0901

꣮	꣯	꣰	꣱	
U1CEE	U1CEF	U1CF0	U1CF1	

It is noticed that these symbols are simply variants in ancient handwriting and printing rather than being distinct in purpose. Sometimes literature uses a combination of any two symbols out of the above to indicate

- *Anusvara facing a sibilant or repha*
- *Anusvara facing a conjunct sibilant*

Visarga Accents

			Accent mark used
अ॓	अ॔	अ॒	
U1CE3	U1CE5	U1CE2	
अ॓ः	अ॔ः	अ॒ः	As seen in print with Visarga (example)
Udatta	Anudatta	Svarita	Accent name
Visarga written with Accents due to various Sandhis.			

Visarga Accents additional due to Sandhi

			Symbols used
अ॔	अ॓		
U1CE4	U1CE7		
अ॔ः	अ॓ः		As seen in print with Visarga (example)
Udatta (mirrored)	Udatta (with tail)		Accent name
Visarga written with such Accent variants is also noticed. However it is more or less a printer's discretion.			

Vowels

अ	आ	इ	ई	
उ	ऊ	ऋ	ॠ	ऌ
ए	ऐ	ओ	औ	

Pluta Vowels

आर	ईर	ऊर	ॠर	Indicates that we have to lengthen the chant
आ३	ई३	ऊ३	ॠ३	
Two ways of writing the same pluta vowel				
ए३	ऐ३	ओ३	औ३	
॥ ओ३म् ॥ अस्माँ३र् *example*				

Consonants (shown with inherent अ vowel)

क	ख	ग	घ	ङ
च	छ	ज	झ	ञ
ट	ठ	ड	ढ	ण
त	थ	द	ध	न
प	फ	ब	भ	म
य	र	ल	व	
श	ष	श	ह	
ळ	ळ्ह	ऱ U097A	Additional consonants seen in the Vedas due to Sandhi

Conjunct Consonants

क्ष	ज्ञ	त्र	ट्ठ	ङ्क
क् ष	ज् ञ	त् र	ट् ठ	ङ् क

Only few samples shown. There are numerous conjunct symbols, formed out of two, three, four or even five consonants without any intervening vowel. These do not have any Unicode, they are made by open type indic shaping in the Devanagari font.

Half Consonants or consonants without vowel

क्	ख्	ग्	घ्	ङ्
च्	छ्	ज्	झ्	ञ्
ट्	ठ्	ड्	ढ्	ण
त्	थ्	द्	ध्	न्
प्	फ	ब्	भ्	म्
य्		ल्	व्	
श्	ष्	स्	ह्	

These symbols are designed by indic shaping features of an open type font and do not have any associated Unicode.

Rigveda Accent Marks

◌̲	◌̍		Accent mark
अ॒	अ॑		Accents as seen in print in presence of vowel. (example)
Anudatta accent to indicate low pitch	Svarita accent to indicate high pitch		Accent meaning. Note that in most Vedic texts, the Udatta or standard pitch is left unmarked.

Rigveda Sandhi Symbols

१॒	hrsva Kampa Sandhi symbol	Short vowel sandhi	मक्षु इत्था = मक्षिव१॒ त्था U0967+0951+0952
३॒	dirgha Kampa Sandhi symbol	Long vowel sandhi	न एव = नेऽ३॒ व U0969+0951+0952
These symbols are made using a sequence of Unicodes.			

Atharvaveda Accents and Sandhi Symbols

अ	अ	⌡	꣱	ꣳ
Anudatta accent to indicate low pitch	Svarita accent to indicate high pitch	Independent Svarita accent - जात्य svarita accent. E.g. तन्वा॑महे or तन्वा॑ऽमहे U1CE1	hrsva Kampa Sandhi symbol – क्षैप्र svarita accent	dirgha Kampa Sandhi symbol – प्रश्लिष्ट / अभिनिहित svarita accent
जात्य svarita accent to indicate genus or species				
क्षैप्र svarita accent occurs for letters that give rise to यण् sandhi				
अभिनिहित svarita accent for diphthongs that give rise to avagraha				
प्रश्लिष्ट svarita accent for letters that give rise to दीर्घ, गुण, or वृद्धि sandhis.				
Since Atharvaveda verses comprise only Rigveda metrical system, so accents and symbols are similar to Rigveda				

Samaveda Accents for Recitation or Singing

Samaveda has two distinct modes of recitation. One is simple chanting and another is singing. The accent marking system differs significantly. In simple chanting the numbers 1, 2, 3 are used to represent Udatta, Svarita, Anudatta respectively. In singing, there are further two sub-systems of marking the accents, in one sub-system the numbers 1 to 5 are used, and in another the numbers 1 to 7 are used, to represent tones of the musical scale. Further, in both systems the letters उ , र , क are additionally used to show sandhi due to change in accent. Moreover र is independently used to show that vowel is long and chanted accordingly.

Samaveda Accents and Sandhi Symbols

१ ◌	२ ◌	३ ◌	Accent mark
UA8E1	UA8E2	UA8E3	
१ अ	२ अ	३ अ	Accent marks seen in print in presence of vowel
Udatta	Svarita	Anudatta	accent meaning
२ उ ◌◌	२उ अ		Svarita accent when lost, a sandhi mark for sequence Udatta+Udatta+Anudatta.
२ र ◌◌	२र अ		Svarita accent when preceded by Udatta, a sandhi mark for sequence Udatta+Udatta+Svarita.
३ क ◌◌	३क अ		Anudatta accent when followed by Svarita, a sandhi mark for sequence Anudatta+Svarita.

Samaveda Singing Accents and Sandhi Symbols - alternate system when sung (corresponding to the standard musical scale from Yajnavalkya Shiksha text)

Accent Mark	Musical Scale 1 to 7	Sama note name	Resembles the call of

१	म ma	मध्यम	heron
२	ग ga	गान्धार	goat
३	ऋ ri	ऋषभ	bull
४	सा sa	षड्ज	peacock
५	घ dha	धैवत	horse

Samaveda Singing texts show only the above accents

६	नि ni	निषाद	elephant
	प pa	पञ्चम	koel

सप्त स्वराः, त्रयो ग्रामा, मूर्छनास्त्वेकविंशतिः । ताना एकोनपञ्चाशत्, इत्येतत्स्वरमण्डलम्

(नारदीयशिक्षायाम्)

सामस्वराणां निर्णयो नारदीयशिक्षायां सामविधानब्राह्मणे चैवं दृश्यते—

यः सामगानां प्रथमः स वेणोर्मध्यमः स्वरः । यो द्वितीयः स गान्धारः, तृतीयस्त्वृषभः स्मृतः ।
चतुर्थः षड्ज इत्याहुः, पञ्चमो धैवतो भवेत् । षष्ठो निषादो विज्ञेयः, सप्तमः पञ्चमः स्मृतः ॥

(नारदीयशिक्षायाम्)

Shukla Yajurveda Accents and Anusvara Symbols

꣺				Accents
svarita	svarita	svarita	svarita (or anudatta)	
U1CD5	U1CD6	U1CD7	U1CD8	
anusvara	anusvara	anusvara	anusvara	anusvara
U1CEA	U1CEC	U1CEE	U1CEF	U1CF0

Shatapatha Brahmana Accents and Symbols

꣺				य

यद्देवु देवतायाऽ आदिश्गति। श्रावतीभ्यो ह वै देवताभ्यो हवींष्यपि गृह्न्तऽ ऋणसु हैव तास्तेन मन्यन्ते बुदस्मै तं कामꣳसमर्द्धयेयुर्यंत्काम्यागृह्लाति तुस्माद्दे देवतायाऽ आदिशत्येवुमेवु यथापूर्व्वꣳ हवींष्यपि गृहीत्वा॥ १९ ॥

(त्यु) अथ सन्न्हनं व्युत्त ꣵ सयति। प्रक्ळत ꣵ दैवास्य स्त्री विजायत ऽइति तुस्मात्सन्न्हनं व्युत्त ꣵ सयति तद्दक्षिणायाꣵ श्रोणो निदधाति नीविद्धैंवास्यैषा दक्षिणत्र ऽइवु हीयं नीविस्तुस्माद्दक्षिणायाꣳ श्रोणौ निदधाति तत्पुनरभिच्छादयत्यभिच्छत्रेवु हीयं नीविस्तुस्मात्पुनरभिच्छादयति ॥ ६ ॥

Krishna Yajurveda Kathaka Samhita Accent Marking System

There are four accents, namely Udatta, Anudatta, Svarita and

Prachaya.

- Udatta is marked with a vertical line on top.
- Anudatta is left unmarked.
- Svarita is of three types, marked with a dot below, marked with underscore, and marked with small-omega below.
- Prachaya is left unmarked.

	Udatta accent		Generally this symbol is a Svarita, however Udatta in Kathaka Samhita
	Svarita accent		इषे त्वोर्जे त्वा ।
	Jatya Svarita accent	Preceded by Anudatta	Generally this symbol is an Anudatta, however Svarita in Kathaka
	Jatya Svarita accent	When preceded by Udatta	वरुणः पस्त्यास्वा

Krishna Yajurveda - Independent Anusvara Sandhi Symbols

	Chanted as गुँ "gum"		Anusvara followed by sibilants or repha (श ष स ह , र)
	Chanted as ग्ग् "gg"		Anusvara followed by a conjunct that begins with a sibilant (श ष स ह)

| | UA8F3+0951 | Svarita Accented Nasalization "gum" |
| | UA8F3+0952 | Anudatta Accented Nasalization "gum" |

Krishna Yajurveda Maitrayani Samhita - Accents and Symbols

III	Svarita accent		Svarita variant symbol in another print edition
U1CDB		U1CD5	
	Svarita Accent		Svarita variant symbol in another print edition
U1CD4		U1CD6	
	Svarita Accent		Svarita variant symbol in another print edition
U1CD7		U1CD8	

Manuscript Text Plates

Here we list the Unicode characters for the special Vedic Symbols and a sample manuscript text with its page number.

Rigveda Samhita – Delhi Sanskrit Academy

꣒ U+0952, ꣑ U+0951, ळ U+0933 ँ U+0901 Page 1

ऋग्वेदसंहिता

[शाकलशाखा]

अथ प्रथमोऽष्टकः   अथ प्रथमं मण्डलम्

प्रथमोऽध्यायः   प्रथमोऽनुवाकः

(१) प्रथमं सूक्तम्

(१-९) नवर्चस्यास्य सूक्तस्य वैश्वामित्रो मधुच्छन्दा ऋषिः । अग्निर्देवता । गायत्री छन्दः ॥

वर्गः

॥ १ ॥ अग्निमीळे पुरोहितं यज्ञस्य देवमृत्विजम्   । होतारं   रत्नधातमम् ॥ १ ॥

अग्निः पूर्वेभिर्ऋषिभिरीड्यो नूतनैरुत   । स देवाँ एह वक्षति ॥ २ ॥

३꣑꣒ (sequence U+0969 U+0951 U+0952) Page 16

नि षसाद धृतव्रतो वरुणः पस्त्या३ःस्वा   । साम्राज्याय   सुक्रतुः ॥ १० ॥

ळ्ह (sequence U+0933 U+094D U+0939) Page 25

अ. १ अ. ३ व. ४-५]   ऋग्वेदः   [म. १ अनु. ७ सू. ३४ २५

न्याविध्यदिलीबिशस्य दृळ्हा वि शृङ्गिणमभिनच्छुष्णमिन्द्रः ।

१꣑꣒ (sequence U+0967 U+0951 U+0952) Page 38

३८ अ. १ अ. ४ व. ४-५]   ऋग्वेदः   [म. १ अनु. ९ सू. ४८

आ घा योषेव सूनर्युषा याति प्रभुञ्जती   ।

जरयन्ती वृजनं पद्वदीयत उत्पातयति पक्षिणः   ॥ ५ ॥

॥ ४ ॥ वि या सृजति समनं व्यर्थिनः पदं न वेत्योदती   ।

Rigveda Samhita – Satvalekar / Delhi Sanskrit Academy

॒ U+0952, ॑ U+0951, ꣶ U+A8F6 Page 750 / 833

ऋग्वेदः। अ० ८, अ० ८, व० ४] [७५०] [मं० १०, सू० १४६, मं० १

(१४६)

६ ऐरम्मदो देवमुनिः । अरण्यानी । अनुष्टुप् ।

अर॑ण्यान्यर॑ण्या॒न्य॒सौ या प्रेव॒ नश्य॑सि ।
क॒था ग्राम॒ं न पृ॑च्छसि॒ न त्वा॒ भीरि॑व विन्दतीꣶ १

[१४६] षट्चत्वारिंशदुत्तरशततमं सूक्तम्
ऋषिः – देवमुनिरैरम्मदः ॥ देवता – अरण्यानी ॥ छन्दः – १ विराडनुष्टुप्; २ भुरिग् अनुष्टुप्; ३, ५ निचृदनुष्टुप्; ४, ६ अनुष्टुप् ॥ स्वरः – गान्धारः ॥

॥४॥ अर॑ण्यान्यर॑ण्यान्य॒सौ य प्रेव॒ नश्य॑सि ।
क॒था ग्राम॒ं न पृ॑च्छसि॒ न त्वा॒ भीरि॑व विन्दतीꣶ ॥ १ ॥

Atharvaveda Paippalada Samhita – Raghu Vira

ᳲ U+1CF2 Page 6

१.२१

नामन्त्रसंस्वयंस्त्रसंन्? असतीभ्यो असत्तराः ।
सेहोर् अरसतरा लवणाद् विक्लेदीयसीः ॥१॥
अपचितᳲ प्र पतत सुपर्णो वसतेर् इव ।
सूर्यᳲ कृणोतु भेषजं चन्द्रमा वो [अ]पोच्छतु ॥२॥

॑ U+0951, ᳜ U+1CDC, ᳝ U+1CDD, ᳲ U+1CF2 Page 7

१.२५

हि॑रण्यवर्णा॑श्᳜ शु॑च᳝यᳲ पाव᳜का॑ [या॑]सु᳝ जा॑तᳲ क᳜श्य॑पो या॑स्व् इन्द्र᳝ः ।
या॑ ᳜अ॒ग्नि॑ गर्भ᳝॑ दधि॑रे᳜ सुव॑र्णा᳜स् ता॑ न᳜ आ॑पश्᳜ शं॑ स्यो᳜ना॑ भ᳝वन्तु ॥१॥

१̣ , ३̣ (sequence U0967+0951+0952)

८३ ब्रह्मचर्य से मृत्यु का नाश ।

ब्रह्मचर्येण तपसा देवा मृत्युमुपाघ्नत ।

इन्द्रो॑ ह ब्रह्मचर्येण देवेभ्यः स्वरा॑भरत्॥१६

८२ कन्या का ब्रह्मचर्य ।

ब्रह्मचर्येण कन्या॑ युवा॑नं विन्दते पति॑म् ।

अनड्वान् ब्रह्मचर्येणाश्वो॑ घासं जिगीर्षति॥१८

Atharvaveda Samhita – Satvalekar

ʃ U+1CE1, ◌̐ U+0951, ◌̱ U+0952

विद्या श॒रस्य॑ पि॒तरः॑ प॒र्जन्यं॑ भूरि॑धायसम् ।
वि॒द्मो ष्व॑स्य मा॒तरः॑ पृ॒थि॒वीं भूरि॑वर्प॑सम्॥ १ ॥
ज्याʃ के॒ परि॑ णो न॒माश्मा॑नं त॒न्वं॑ ʃ कृधि ।
वी॒डुर्व॒री॒योऽ रा॑ति॒रप॒ द्वेषा॑ᳵस्या कृधि॥ २ ॥

∫ U+1CE1 , ॑ U+0951, ॒ U+0952

अथर्ववेदसंहिता

अथ प्रथमं काण्डम्

अथ प्रथमः प्रपाठकः

अथ प्रथमोऽनुवाकः [१] प्रथमं सूक्तम्

ऋषिः—अथर्वा ॥ देवता—वाचस्पतिः ॥ छन्दः—१-३ अनुष्टुप्;
४ चतुष्पदाविराडुरोबृहती ॥

ये त्रिषप्ताः परियन्ति विश्वा रूपाणि बिभ्रतः ।
वाचस्पतिर्बला तेषाᳵ तन्वो ∫ अद्य दधातु मे ॥१॥

꣡ U+A8E1, ꣢ U+A8E2, ꣣ U+A8E3, ꣢꣯ U+A8E2+A8EF,

꣢꣫ U+A8E2+A8EB, ꣣꣬ U+A8E3+A8EC Page 1, 2, 5

१.   अग्र आ याहि

नि होता सत्सि

आदित्प्रत्नस्य रेतसो ज्योतिः पश्यन्ति वासरम् । परो यदिध्यते दिवि ॥ १० ॥

५२.   अध ज्मो अध वा दिवो

अया वर्धस्व तन्वा गिरा

◌̂ U+1CD0, ◌̄ U+1CD2

कस्यानू१ना२म् । परोषा२३४सी । धियोजिन्वा२ ।

सिस्त्या२३४नाइ । गोषाताया२३ । ख्यार्ता२३४औचो-

वा । उप् । गो२३४रा: ॥ २० ॥ ३३

उचाता२इइजातमन्धसा: । दिवाइसा ऽ१ङ् र२ ।

द्युँ स्त्राँ नाँ ऽ२इइमा र२ ।

८४   सामवेदसंहिता ।   [१म प्र०, १म अ०

मैषा प्रथमा ।

* अग्न॒त्रा या॑हि वी॒तये॑ ग्रणा॒नोह॑व्यदा॒तये॑ ।

नि होता॑ सत्सि॒ बर्हिषि॑ ॥ १ ॥

१० अोग्ना इ । अायाचो२ वोइतोया २इ । तोया२इ ।

गृणानोह । व्यदातोया २इ । तोया २इ । ना इच्होतासा

◌ U+A8E1, ◌ U+A8E2, ◌ U+A8E3, ◌ U+A8E4, ◌ U+A8E5, ◌ U+A8EF

III ओग्निः । वृचाणि जड्डनात् । औचौचो२३४ वा ।

द्रविणस्युर्विपन्यया । औचौचो२३४वा । समिद्धः शुक्र

या । औचौचो२३४वा । चोधूतो५५चायि ॥ ८ ॥४

Samaveda Uha Uhya Ganam Vol 1 – Sringeri

◌ U+A8E0, ◌ U+A8E1, ◌ U+A8E2, ◌ U+A8ED, ◌ U+A8EF

Page 166, 167

का गृणानोह्=गृणानोह् ।

खी ष्णवा५३इ ॥

घ.नामत्वष्टुरपीचियामियाउवा२रइहोवा२रइहा२रईया ॥ घा. मधोअर्षन्तिधार-
याउवाहोवाहो प्रे ईया=मधोअर्षन्तिधारयाउवा२रइहोवा२रइहा२रईया२र । धि.

ङ.=सूनु ७ सत्या५३१२३ ॥ ज=आभिवत्सा५३१२३४मृ ॥ झि. धियाङ्क-
णयानओवा२३ओ५३४वा ॥ झी आ५शुमतीमतिष्ठा५रत् ॥ ञ पू२रदधिषो५३४-

इन्द्रे विन्स्सोमा विन् सहइ=इन्द्रे५रसोमा५रससहइ ॥ ञः- त्वंवृत्राणिह्५यप्रतीन्येक-
इतपुरू ।

माऽ३परि । षाऽ३४३इ । च्याऽ३माऽ५"नाऽ६५६: ॥ श्री: ॥

एवापवा । स्वाऽ३मदि । रोमदाया ॥ उद्ग्राभा । स्याऽ३नम । यन्व-

घस्नूम् ॥ परिवर्णम् । भरमा । णोरुशन्ताम् ॥ औहोवाहाऽ३होइ ।

इहा । गव्युनोंआ । षाऽ३परि । सोऽ३४३ । माऽ३साऽ५"काऽ६५६: ॥

दी. २१. उत्. १८. मा. २४. गी. ॥४२॥

३. श्यैतम् ॥ प्रजापति: । बृहती । इन्द्र: ।

अभिप्रवस्सुरा । घसाऽ३४औहोवा ॥ आइन्द्रमर्च । यथाविदा-

ऽ२३४इ । ओऽ६हा । योजरित्रृभ्य: । माघाऽ२३वा । पुरूऽ२र । वाऽ२३४-

236

◌ U+1CF2, Page 198

इति तृतीय: खरुड:

१०. प्र । तु । द्रव । परि । कोशाम् । नि । सीद । नृभि: । पुनान: ।

४. औशानम् ॥ उशना: । त्रिष्टुप् । पवमान: सोम: ।

प्रातू ॥ द्रवापरिकोशाम् । निषोऽ३दा । नृभाइऽपुना । नोऽ३ अभि ।

72

च्याऽ३माऽ५"नाऽ६५६:

सोऽ३४३ । माऽ३साऽ५इ"काऽ६५६: ॥
दी. २१. उत्. १८. मा. २४. गी. ॥४२॥

झ-घर्मे ꣼प्रवृक्तस्तन्वासमानृधेवृधेसुवाऽर३४५: ॥ झा-अर्कस्यदेवाꣳ परमेबियो-
विन्मान्-अर्कस्यदेवा ꣼परमेबियोऽरमाऽर३४५न् ॥ क्षि-नत्वदन्योमघबाऽर३नाऽर ।
झी-रिपुरीक्षीतमाऽ३१उवाऽर२ ॥ झु-तक्षद्यदाऽर२१२३४इ ॥ झू-द्रवाससाऽर१उवाऽर-
३४५ । झे-ख्येअन्धसाऽर: ॥ झै-तवेदसाऽर२३म् ॥ झो-सपर्यवायेऽ३४ ॥ झौ ई अ
न्द्रंवायाप्रेम्=इन्द्रंवायाऽर२म् ॥ झम् र अ रा=रराऽर३ ॥ झः-जाअनानाम्=जनाऽ-
र३नाम् ॥

याम्=पावऽ२रेकाश ꣳ साऽर२३याम् ॥ षै-बावऽ२रेताइवृत्राहाऽर२३४न् ॥ षो-प्रतेधारा-
मधुमऽ२रेताइरस्तृमाऽर२३४५न् ॥ षौ-उत्त्राताशिबोसुबः ॥ षम्=प्रभुगोत्राणिपरियेषि-
विश्वताऽर२३: ॥ षः-हृत्यहसम्भ्योजायमानाऽर२३४: ॥

स-वाजीजिगीवाविश्वाधना विन् नी=वाजीजिगीवाविश्वाधनाऽरनीऽर२३४५ ॥
सा-घर्मे ꣼प्रवृक्तस्तन्वासमानशेमहेसुवाऽर२३४५: ॥ सि-ईयान ꣼कृष्णोदशभिस्सहस्रै: ॥

ड-पिर्बाऽ३४तुवाऽर ॥ डा-महाऽ३४३मृविपोधाम् ॥ डि-कदाऽ३४औ-
होवा । डी-अहाऽ३१२न्याऽर३४द्वा ॥ डु-औहोऽ३रेहाऽ३ ॥ डू-वियञ्जतेसमञ्जते ॥
डे-अस्तिसोमोअयꣳसुतः ॥ डै-इन्द्रमच्छसुताइमेवृषण्यन्तुहा ॥ डो-थिनाशवाऽर२-
२२३४३: । डौ-उपोपेन्नुमघवन्भूयइत् ॥

Shukla Yajurveda Kanva Samhita - Satvalekar

ळ U+0933

शिव रुतस्यं भेषजी तया नो मृळ जीवसें ॥३॥

यजंमानस्य परिधिरंस्यग्निरिळ ईळितः ।

Shukla Yajurveda Vajasaneyi Samhita

⸲ U+1CE2 (after U+0903)

नमस्ते रुद्र मुन्यवंऽउतो तऽइषंवे नमंः । बाहुंभ्यामुत ते नमंः ॥१॥

Vajasaneyi Madhyandina Samhita. 16th Chapter. Verse 1.

Shukla Yajurveda Rudrashtadhyayi – Gita Press

⸲ U+1CE2, ⸳ U+1CE3, ⸵ U+1CE5 (after U+0903)

ॐ अबोद्ध्यग्निः समिधाजनानाम्प्रतिधेनुमिवायतीमुषासम् ।
यह्वाऽ इवप्रवयामुज्जिहानाः प्रभानवंः सिस्त्रतेनाकमच्छ ॥

यत्प्रज्ञानमुतचेतोधृतिश्चयज्ज्योतिरन्तरमृतम्प्रजासु ॥ यस्मान्नऽऋते-
किञ्चनकर्म्मक्रियतेतन्मेमनंःशिवसंङ्कल्पमस्तु ॥७॥ येनेदम्भूतम्भुव-
नम्भविष्यत्परिगृहीतममृतेनसर्व्वम् ॥ येनयज्ञस्तायतेसप्तहोतातन्मेमनंः
शिवसंङ्कल्पमस्तु ॥८॥ यस्मिन्नृचऽसामयजुंःऽषियस्मिन्प्रतिष्ठि-
तारथनाभाविवारा? ॥ यस्मिँश्चित्तःसर्व्वमोतम्प्रजानान्तन्मेमनंःशिव-
संङ्कल्पमस्तु ॥९॥ सुषारथिरश्श्वानिवयन्मनुष्यान्नेनीयतेभीशुभिर्व्वाजिन-
ऽइव ॥ हृत्प्रतिष्ठं यदजिरञ्जविष्ठन्तन्मेमनंःशिवसंङ्कल्पमस्तु ॥१०॥

॥ इति रुद्रपाठे प्रथमोऽध्यायः ॥ १ ॥

पादाऽउच्च्येते ।।१०।। ब्राह्मणोऽस्यमुखमासीद्वाहूराजन्य्ऽहृकृतः ।। उ

स्यर्यद्वैश्यः पद्भ्याँऽशूद्द्रोऽअजायत ।।११।। चन्द्रमामनसोजातश्

सूर्व्योऽअजायत ।। श्रोत्राद्वायुश्श्चप्राणश्श्चमुखादग्निरजायत ।।

नाभ्याऽआसीदन्तरिक्षꣳ शीष्ण्र्ोद्यौश्समवर्त्तत ।। पद्भ्याम्भूमिर्दिशꣳ

विदंव्वज्रबाहुꣳयर्यन्तमज्जꣳयप्रमृणन्तमोजसा ।। इमꣳ संजाताऽअनुवीरय

दध्वमिन्द्रꣳ सखायोऽअनुसꣳरभद्ध्वम् ।।६।। अभिगोत्राणिसहसा

रुद्राष्टाध्यायी

——— प्रथमोऽध्यायः ———

श्रीगणेशाय नमः ।। हरिः ॐ गुणानान्त्वागणपतिꣳहवामहे

प्रियाणान्त्वाप्रियपतिꣳहवामहेनिधीनान्त्वानिधिपतिꣳ हवामहेव्वसोमम ।

आहमजानिगर्भधमात्त्वमजासिगर्भधम् ।।१।। गायत्रीत्रिष्टुब्जगत्यनुष्टु-

प्पङ्क्चासह । बृहत्युष्णिहाककुप्प्सूचीभिꣳशम्य्न्तुत्त्वा ।।२।।

Shukla Yajurveda Rudrashtadhyayi –

र्वाभिजगंदयक्ष्मꣳ सुमनास्त्रसंत् ॥ ४ ॥

त्र्यंयंवोचदधिवक्का प्रथमोदैव्योभिषक् ॥

अहीꣳश्च सर्वाञ्जम्भयन्त्सर्वाꣳश्च यातुधान्यो

धराचीःपरासुव ॥ ५ ॥ असौयस्ताम्रोऽअरु

णऽउतबभ्रुꣳ सुमङ्गलः ॥ येचैनꣳ रुद्राऽ

अभितोदिक्षुश्रिताꣳसहस्रशोवैषा हेडईमहे ॥ ६ ॥ असौयोऽवसर्पतिनीलग्रीवोविलो

हितः ॥ उतैनंगोपाऽअदृश्रन्नदृश्रन्नुदहार्यः ॥

ॐ आशुःशिशानोवृषभोन भीमोघनाघ

नऽऽऽआभंगाश्चर्षणीनाम् । सङ्क्रन्दनोनिमिष

ऽएकवीरऽशतꣳ सेनाऽऽअजयत्साकमिन्द्रः ॥ १ ॥ सङ्क्रन्दनेनानिमिषेणजिष्णुनायुत्का

नस्त्वमुभयोरात्न्योंज्र्याम् ॥ याश्चतेहस्तऽ

इषवऽपरातांभगवोवप ॥ २ ॥ द्विज्यन्धनुः

कपर्दिनो विशल्ल्यो बाणंवाँ २ ऽउत ॥

अनेशन्नस्ययाऽइषवऽआभुरस्यनिषङ्ग विऽ

Shukla Yajurveda Rudrashtadhyayi – Khemraj

꠰ U+0952, ꠱ U+0951, ꠱ U+1CD8, ꠱ U+1CD6, ꠱ U+1CE2,

꠱ U+1CE4, ꠱ U+1CD5, ꠱ U+1CF0, य U+097A   Page 54, 55

अवतत्त्यधनुष्ट्वर्ँसहस्राक्षशतेषुधे ॥ निशीय्यँद्र
ल्यानाम्मुखाँशिवोनँसुमनाँभव ॥ १२ ॥

मानोंमहान्तमुतमानोँऽअर्भकम्मानऽउक्षन्तमु-
तमानऽउक्षितम् ॥ मानोँवधीःपितरम्मोतमात-
रम्मानँप्रियास्तन्वोरुद्ररीरिषः ॥ १५ ॥

Shukla Yajurveda - Loose Leaf – Khemraj

꠱ U+1CD8, ꠱ U+1CEE, ꠱ U+1CE9, ꠱ U+0951, य U+097A

꠱ U+1CE2, ꠱ U+1CE5, ꠱ U+1CE6, ꠱ U+1CE7, ꠱ U+1CE8,(after U+0903)

꠱ U+1CF1 Page 427

स्युनाभिमश्श्वँऽअज्ञानँसरिरस्युमध्यें ॥ शिशुन्वदीनाँहरिमद्रिबु
ध्रमग्रेमाहिँसीःपरमेव्योँमन् ॥ ४२ ॥ अजस्त्रमिन्दुम् ॥ अजस्त्र
मिन्दुमरुपम्भुरण्युमग्निर्मीडेपूर्वांचित्तिमाँभिः ॥ सपर्व्वभिर्ऋतुशँ
कल्पमानोगाम्माहिँसीरादितित्रिराजम् ॥ ४३ ॥ वरूत्रिन्त्वश्शुँ ॥
वरूत्रिन्त्वश्वरुणस्युनाभिमविँऽअज्ञानाँरजसुँपरस्म्मात् ॥ मुही
ँसाहस्त्रिमसुरस्यमायायामग्रेमाहिँसीःपरमेव्योँमन ॥ ४४ ॥ योऽ
अग्निः ॥ योऽअग्निरग्भेरद्घचजाँयतुशोकात्पृथिव्याऽउतवादिवस्प्प
रि ॥ येनप्रजाविश्वकम्माँजुजानतमग्नेहेडःपरितेवृणक्क् ॥ ४५ ॥

Shukla Yajurveda Vajasaneyi – Delhi Sanskrit Academy

☯ U+1CE9, ♒ U+0951, ♒ U+0952, ✬ U+A8F3 Page 89

नीलग्रीवाः शितिकण्ठा दिवꣳरुद्राऽ उपश्रिताः।

तेषाꣳꣶसहस्रयोजनेऽव धन्वानि तन्मसि॥५६॥

Shukla Yajurveda Vajasaneyi Madhyandina Samhita –

♘ U+1CD8, ♯ U+1CEF, ☯ U+1CE9, ♒ U+0951, य U+097A

♣ U+1CE3, ♥ U+1CE5,(after U+0903) Page Chapter 16

ये चैनꣷ रुद्राऽअभितो दिक्षु श्रिश्रिताः सहस्रशोवैषाꣴ हेडईमहे ॥६॥

असौ योवसर्पति नीलग्रीवो विलोहित꣱ ।

Shukla Yajurveda Vajasaneyi Madhyandina Samhita –

♘ U+1CD8, ♰ U+1CF0, ♒ U+0951, ♢ U+1CE2 (after U+0903) Page

हरिꣲꣳꣳꣴऀ ॐ ॥ गुणानान्त्वागुणपतिꣶꣵहवामहेप्रियाणान्त्वा

प्रियपतिꣶꣵहवामहेनिधीनान्त्वानिधिपतिꣶꣵहवामहेव -

सोमम ॥ आह   मंजानिगर्भधमात्त्वमंजासिगर्भु

धम ॥ १ ॥

Shukla Yajurveda Samhita –

♖ U+1CD6, ♘ U+1CD8, ♯ U+1CEF, ☯ U+1CE9, ♒ U+0951, य U+097A

♢ U+1CE2, ♣ U+1CE3, ♥ U+1CE5,(after U+0903) Page

विष्णणोꣳश्त्रप्त्रैस्स्थोविष्णणोꣳस्यूरसिविष्णणोंद्धु
वोऽसि। वैष्णणवर्मसिविष्णणवेत्वा॥३६९॥ ब्रह्म-
मन्त्रः—ॐ ब्ब्रह्मजज्ञानम्प्रथमम्पुरस्ताद्द्विसीमतः
सुरुचौविनऽआवः। सबुध्ध्न्याऽउपुमाऽअस्यविष्ठाः
सतश्च्योनिमसतश्च्विर्वः॥३७०॥ इन्द्रमन्त्रः— ॐ
त्रातारमिन्द्रमवितारमिन्द्रꣳ हवेहवेसुहवꣳ शूरमिन्द्रम्।
ह्वयामिशक्क्रम्पुरुहूतमिन्द्रꣳस्वस्तिर्नोꣳमघवाधा
त्विन्द्रः॥३७१॥ यममन्त्रः—ॐ यमायत्त्वामुखाय

उपयामगृहीतोऽसीन्द्राय त्वा बृहद्द्वते वयस्वतऽउक्थाव्यं
गृह्णामि। यत्तऽइन्द्र बृहद्द्वयस्तस्मै त्वा विष्णवे त्वैष ते योनि-
रुक्थेभ्यस्त्वा देवेभ्यस्त्वा देवाव्यं यज्ञस्यायुषे गृह्णामि ॥२२॥

Shukla Yajurveda Vajasaneyi Samhita – Khemraj

꣑ U+0951, ꣷ U+1CD8, ꣵ U+A8F5, ꣥ U+1CE5, ꣯ U+1CEF

Page 401, 5th Chapter, Page 406, 7th Chapter

देव सवितरेष ते सोमस्त्तꣳ रक्षस्व मा त्वा दभन्। एतत्त्वन्देव सोम देवो देवाꣳऽ
उपागाऽइदमहम्मनुष्प्यान्त्सुह रायस्प्पोषेण स्वाहा निर्वरुणस्यु पाशान्मुच्ये ॥३९॥

॥१०॥ उरु विष्णणो विक्क्रमस्वोरु क्षयाय नस्कृधि।
घृतꣷतयोने पिबु प्प्रप्र युज्ज्ञपतिन्तिर स्वाहा ॥४१॥
अत्युन्या रँ॥ऽअगान्त्राह्या रँ॥ऽउपागामुर्वाक्त्वा परेꣵभ्योविदम्पुरोवरेꣵभ्यꣳ। तन्त्वा
जुषामहे देव व्वनस्प्पते देवयज्ञ्यायै देवास्त्वा देवयज्ञ्यायै जुषन्ताꣳविष्णणवे त्वा।
ओषधे त्रायस्व स्वधिते मैनꣳ हिꣳसीꣳ ॥४२॥

॥२४॥ मुहा रँ॥ऽइन्द्रो यऽओजसा पर्जन्यो वृष्टिमा रँ॥ऽइव। स्तोमैर्व्वत्सस्य बावृधे। उपुया
मगृहीतोसि महेन्द्राय त्वैष ते योनिम्महेन्द्राय त्वा ॥४०॥

कृष्णमन्यद्धरितःसम्भरन्ति॥१२॥बण्महाँ ३ँ असिसूर्य्यं
बडांदित्यमहाँ ३ँ असि महस्तेसतो महिमार्पन-
स्यतेद्धादैवमहाँ ३ँ असि ॥ १३ ॥ बदसूर्य्यश्रवं-
सामहाँ ३ँ असि सत्रांदंवमहाँ ३ँ असिमहृादेवा-

Nityakarma Prayogamala (Khemraj)

Krishna Yajurveda Kathaka Samhita

☉ U+1CDD Page

इषे त्वोर्जे त्वा ।

Krishna Yajurveda Kathaka Samhita

☉ U+1CD5 Page

[२]   काठक-संहितायाम्   [स्थानकं १, अनु॰ २-६ मं. १२-२१

मातरिश्वनो घर्मोंऽसि द्यौरसि पृथिव्युसि विश्वधायाः परेण धाम्नाहुतासि मा ह्वास्सा विश्वा-
युस्सा विश्वग्यचास्सा विश्वधाया हुतंस्तोकौं हुतौ द्रप्सोऽग्रये बृहतै नाकाय स्वाहा द्यावापृथि-
वीभ्याम् ॥   १२

Krishna Yajurveda Kathaka Samhita – Satvalekar

देवस्य त्वा सवितुः प्रसवेऽश्विनोर्बाहुभ्यां पूष्णो हस्ताभ्यामाददे गोपदसि प्रत्युष्टं रक्षः प्रत्युष्ट-
रातिः प्रेयमगाद्द्विषणा बहिरञ्छ मनुना कृता स्वधया वितष्ठा ॥ उर्वन्तरिक्षं वीहीन्द्रस्य परिघृतमसि
माधौ मौपरि परस्त ऋध्यासमाच्छेत्ता ते मा रिषत् ॥ देव बर्हिशतवलशं विरोह सहस्रवलशा वि
चयं रुहेम ॥ अदित्या रास्नासीन्द्राण्यास्संनहनं पूषा ते ग्रन्थि ग्रथ्नातु स ते मा स्थादिन्द्रस्य त्वा
बाहुभ्यामुद्यच्छे बृहस्पतेस्त्वा मूर्ध्नोहरामि देवज्ञमसि ॥ तदाहरन्ति कवयः पुरस्तादेवेभ्यो जुष्टमिह
बर्हिरासदे ॥ २ ॥

५–९

Krishna Yajurveda Maitrayani Samhita – Satvalekar

॥ ॐ ॥ इषे त्वा सुभूताय, वायव स्थ, देवो वः सविता प्रार्पयतु श्रेष्ठतमाय कर्मणा,
आप्यायध्वमघ्या देवेभ्या इन्द्राय भागे, मा व स्तेन ईशत माघशꣳसो ध्रुवा अस्मिन्
गोपतौ स्यात बह्वीं, —यजमानस्य पशून् पाहि ॥ १ ॥

१

अयुपिता यौनि, —रदित्या रास्नासीन्द्राण्याः संनहनं, पूषा ते ग्रन्थि ग्रथ्नातु, स ते मो
स्यादि, —न्द्रस त्वा बाहुभ्यामुद्यच्छे, बृहस्पतेर्मूर्ध्नोहराम्यु३, —र्वन्तरिक्षꣳ वी, —रादित्या-
स्त्वा पृष्ठे सादयामि ॥२॥

६

[१८] मैत्रायणी-संहितायाम् [कां०१,प्रपा०२,अनु०३९;प्रपा०४,अनु०१

अवभृथ निचुङ्कुण निचेरुरसि निचुङ्कुणो, गृहै गृहौ, —ऽव नो देवैर्देवकृतमेनो यक्ष्य, —व
मर्त्यैर्मर्त्यकृतं चिकित्वा, —ऽनुरौरा नो देव रिषस्पाह्, —प्सु धौतस्य ते देव सोमनृभिष्टुतस्य यस्ते
गोसनिर्भक्षो यो अश्वसनिस्तस्यु ता उपहूता उपहूतस्य भक्षयामि, विचृत्तो वरुणस्य पाश:,
प्रत्यस्तो वरुणस्य पाशो, नमो वरुणस्य पाशायौ, —त्रेतर्वेशीयो ना उद्बुयाभिः ॥

११९

अथ चतुर्थं काण्डम् ।

अथ प्रथमः प्रपाठकः ।

पुरोडाशब्राह्मणम् ।

वनस्पतीन्वा उग्रो देवं उदौषत्, वं श्शम्यां अध्वशमयं श्, स्वंच् शम्यां: शमीतरं श्, यंच् शमीशाखंयो वृत्सानुपाक्रोति शान्त्यै, पूर्णवती कार्या, पशूनां श्वा एवंरूपं, पशुमान् भवति,

---

Krishna Yajurveda Taittiriya Samhita – Anandashram

◌॑ U+0951, ◌॒ U+0952, ꣳ U+A8F3, ꣴ U+A8F4 Page 1972, 1973

Namakam = Kanda 4 Prapathaka 5 Anuvaka 1

कश्शिहि । यामिषुं गिरिशंत हस्तें (१) बिभर्ष्यस्तवे । शिवां गिरित्र तां कुरु मा हिꣳसीः पुरुषं जगत् । शिवेन वचसा त्वा गिरिशाच्छा वदामसि । यथा नः सर्वमिज्जग-दयक्ष्मꣳ सुमना असत् । अध्यवोचदधिवक्ता

(नित्याग्निहोमोक्तिः)

प्रथमो देव्यो भिषक् । अहीꣳश्च सर्वाञ्जम्भ-यन्त्सर्वाश्च यातुधान्यः । असौ यस्ताम्रो अरुण

82

Krishna Yajurvediya Kathaka Samhita – Satvalekar

꙼ U+0951, ꙳ U+1CD8, ꙷ U+1CD5, ꙰ U+0901 Page 1, 2

VARIANT ACCENT MARKS wrt SCHROEDER

देवस्य त्वा सवितुः प्रसवेऽश्विनोर्बाहुभ्यां पूष्णो हस्ताभ्यामाददे गोपदासि प्रत्युष्टं रक्षः प्रत्युष्टा-
रातिः प्रैयमगाद्द्विषणा बहिरच्छ मनुना कृता स्वधया वितष्ठ ॥ उर्वन्तरिक्षं व्रीहीन्द्रस्य परिषूतमासि
माधो मोपरि परुस्त ऋध्यासमाच्छेत्ता ते मा रिषत् ॥ देव बर्हिश्शतवलशं विरोह सहस्रवलशा वि
वयं रुहेम ॥ अदित्या रक्षासीन्द्राण्यास्संनहनं पूषा ते ग्रन्थिं ग्रथ्नातु सं ते मा स्थादिन्द्रस्य त्वा
बाहुभ्यामुद्यच्छे बृहस्पतेस्त्वा मूर्ध्नाहरामि देवज्जमंमासि ॥ तंदाहरन्ति कवयः पुरस्तादेवेभ्यो जुष्टमिह
बहिरासदे ॥ २ ॥   ५–९

मातरिश्वनो घर्मोऽसि द्यौरसि पृथिव्यसि विश्वधायाः परेण धाम्नाहुतासि मा ह्वास्सा विश्वा-
युस्सा विश्वव्यचास्सा विश्वधाया हुतस्तोको हुतो द्रप्सोऽग्रये बृहते नाकाय स्वाहा द्यावापृथि-
वीभ्याम् ॥   १२

संपृच्यध्वमृतावरीरूर्मिणा मधुमत्तमाः । मन्द्रा धनस्य सातयः ॥   १३

इन्द्रस्य त्वा भागं सोमेनातनच्म्यदस्तमासि विष्णवे विष्णो हव्यं रक्षस्वापो जागृत ॥ ३ ॥ १४

Taittiriya Brahmana – Mahadeva Sastri

꙼ U+0951, ꙵ U+0952, ꯳ U+A8F3, ꯴ U+A8F4 Page 1, 4

तैत्तिरीय ब्राह्मणं

भट्टभास्करभाष्यसहितम्.

प्रथमाष्टके

प्रथमप्रश्नः.

हरिः ओम् ॥ ब्रह्म संधत्तं तन्मे जिन्वतम् । क्षत्रꣳ
संधत्तं तन्मे जिन्वतम् । इषꣳ संधत्तं तां मे जिन्वतम् ।
ऊर्जꣳ संधत्तं तां मे जिन्वतम् । रयिꣳ संधत्तं तां मे

धत्तम् । चक्षुर्यज्ञपतये धत्तम् । श्रोत्रँ स्थरश्रोत्रं मे
धत्तम् । श्रोत्रं यज्ञाय धत्तम् । श्रोत्रं यज्ञपतये धत्तम् ।

Kathaka Samhita Vol 1 – Schroeder

◌॑ U+0951, ◌᳗ U+1CD7, ◌᳙ U+1CD9, ◌ऀ U+0900 Page 1, 2

देवस्य त्वा सवितुः प्रसवे ऽश्विनोर्बाहुभ्यां पूष्णो हस्ताभ्यामाददे
गोषदसि प्रत्युषं रक्षः प्रत्युष्टारातिः प्रेयमगाद्विषणा बहिरच्छ मनुना
कृता स्वधया वितष्टा ॥ उर्वन्तरिक्ष[2] वीहीन्द्रस्य परिषूतमसि
मांधो मोपरि परूस्त ऋध्यासमाच्छेत्ता[3] ते मा रिषत् ॥ देव बर्हि-

[I, 3. 4. 5

मातरिश्वनो घर्मो ऽसि द्यौरसि पृथिव्यसि विश्वधायाः परेण धा
ऽऽहुतासि मा द्वासां विश्वायुसां विश्वव्यचासां विश्वधाया हुत
स्तोकां हुतो द्रप्सो ऽमये[1] बृहते नाकाय स्वाहा द्यावापृथि
वीभ्याम् ॥

संपृच्यध्वमृतावरीरुर्मिणा मधुमत्तमाः ।
मन्द्रा धनस्य सातये[2] ॥
इन्द्रस्य त्वा भागँ सोमेनातनच्म्यदत्तमसि विष्णवे विष्णो हव्यं

84

Maitrayani Samhita Vol 4 – Schroeder

◌॑ U+0951, ◌꣺ U+A8FA, ◌ꣲ U+A8F2, ◌᳗ U+1CD7   Page 1 (IV,1,1.1)

वनस्पतीन्वा उग्रो देव उंदौषन्नꣲ शम्यां अध्यशमीयꣲस्तꣲꣲशम्याः
शमील्वꣲ यꣲशमीशाखंया वत्सांनपाकरौति शांन्ये पर्णवती कार्या
पंशूनाꣲ वा एतद्रूपं पशुमांन्भवति यंद्पर्णा स्यांह्राꣲस्य तद्रूपꣲ व-
ज्रो दराडौं वज्रेण पंशूनभिप्रवर्तये तृतीयस्याꣲ वै दिवि सोंम आ-
सीन्नꣲ गायत्री रयेनों भूत्वाहरन्नꣲस्य पर्णमछिद्यत तंतः पर्णो ऽजायत

Madhyandina Satapatha Brahmana – Vedic Yantralaya

◌॒ U+0952, ◌᳞ U+1CDE   Page 3, 12

वैतत्प्रजननं क्रियते ॥ २२ ॥ ब्राह्मणम् ॥ १ ॥

    अथ शूर्पं चाग्निहोत्रहवणीं चादत्ते । कर्मणे यां येपाय वामिति यज्ञो वै कर्म
यज्ञाय हि तस्मादाह कर्मणे वामिति येपाय वामिति येनेष्टीव हि यज्ञम् ॥ १ ॥ अथ

मंनयन्तीति तत आप्त्याः सम्बभूवुस्थितो द्वित एकलः ॥ १ ॥ तऽइन्द्रेय सह
चेरुः । यथेदं ब्राह्मणो राजानमनुचरति स यत्र निश्शीर्पाएं त्वाप्यं विश्वरूपं ज-
घान तस्य हिते ऽपि बुध्यस्य विद्वाञ्चक्षुः शश्वद्धैनं त्रित एव जघानाह्यह तदि-
न्द्रोऽमुच्यत देवो हि सः ॥ २ ॥ तु च हैतऽऊचुः । उपवेमऽपुनो गच्छन्तु येऽ-

Madhyandina Satapatha Brahmana – Albrecht Weber

◌॒ U+0952, ◌᳟ U+1CDF   Page 3, 15
VARIANT ACCENT MARK

ननं मिथुनमिवैतत्प्रजननं क्रियते ॥२२॥ ब्राह्मणम् ॥१॥

    अथ शूर्पं चाग्निहोत्रहवणीं चादत्ते । कर्मणे वां येषाय वामिति यज्ञो वै कर्म
यज्ञाय हि तस्मादाह कर्मणे वामिति येषाय वामिति येवेष्टीव हि यज्ञम् ॥१॥

नयन्तीति तत ब्राह्याः सम्बभूवुस्त्रितो द्वित एकतः ॥१॥ तऽइन्द्रेण सह चेरुः ।
यथेदं ब्राह्मणो राजानमनुचरति स यत्र त्रिशीर्षाणं वाष्ट्रं विश्वरूपं जघान तस्य
हेतेऽपि बध्यस्य विदाञ्चक्रुः शश्वढैनं त्रित एव जघानात्यद् तदिन्द्रोऽमुच्यत दे-
वा द्धि सः ॥२॥ त उ हेतऽऊचुः । उपैविमऽहृनो गहृतु येऽस्य वध्यस्याविदिषु-

Manuscript Text explaining the Accents

There are several शिक्षा Shiksha texts that deal with correct pronunciation of letters and proper recitation of Vedic verses. E.g.

- Rigveda – Paniniya Shiksha
- Samaveda – Naradiya Shiksha
- Yajurveda – Yajnavalkya Shiksha
- Atharvaveda – Manduki Shiksha

साम-शब्द-वाच्यस्य गानस्य स्वरूपमृगच्चरेषु क्रुष्टादिभिः सप्तभिः
स्वरैः अचरविकारादिभिश्च निष्पाद्यते ।   क्रुष्टः प्रथमो द्वितीय

❋ स्वर-स्तोभ-युक्तित्येव पाठः रा॰ सा॰ पुस्तकयोः ।

"गीतिषु सामाख्या" अतः गानसंवलितैर्मन्त्रै: यज्ञयागादिषु उद्गातृभिर्गीयमानत्वात् एष सामवेद उच्यते । सामगायका:, सामगाश्छन्दोगाश्चाप्युच्यन्ते । यद्यपि सामगानविधि: सामान्यसंगीत शास्त्रत: किञ्चित्विलक्षणस्तथापि षड्ज-ऋषभ-गान्धार-मध्यम-पञ्चम-धैवत-निषादाख्यानां सप्तस्वराणां प्रयोगस्तु सामगाने भवत्येव । अत्र सामगाने सप्तस्वराणां प्रयोग: अतीव रमणीयतया कृतोऽवलोक्यते ।

In the singing version of Samaveda, there are 7 types of Accents. The following illustrates the difference for chanting and singing versions from a passage.

"अग्न आ याहि वीतये गृणानो हव्यदातये।
नि होता सत्सि बर्हिषि"। (सा॰ क्र॰ १ प्र॰ १ ख॰ १ ऋ॰)

अथ गानानि त्रीणि, तत्राद्यं गेयगानस्य प्रथमं साम। तदेव पश्यतु तावत्—

"ओग्नायि। आयाही३ वीयितोया२यि। नो
या२यि। गृणानोह। व्यदातो या२यि। नीया२यि।
नायिह्नो तासा२३। हा२यि। वा २३४त्रौ होवा।
ही२३षो। १"

 नारदीय शिक्षा

यः साभगानां प्रथमः स वेणोर्मध्यमः स्वरः।
यो द्वितीयः स गान्धारस्तृतीयस्त्वृषभः स्मृतः॥ १॥

चतुर्थः षड्जइत्याहुः पञ्चमोधैवतो भवेत्।
षष्ठे निषादो विज्ञेयः सप्तमः पञ्चमः स्मृतः॥ २॥

षड्जं वदति मयूरो गावो रम्भन्ति चर्षभः।
अजाविके तु गान्धारं क्रौञ्चो वदति मध्यमम्॥ ३॥

पुष्पसाधारणे काले कोकिलो वक्ति पञ्चमम्।
अश्वस्तु धैवतं वक्ति निषादं वक्ति कुञ्जरः॥ ४॥

जात्यः क्षैप्रोऽभिनिहितस्तैरव्यञ्जन एव च।
तिरोविरामः प्रश्लिष्टः पादवृत्तश्च सप्तमः॥ १०॥

स्वराणामहमेतेषाम् पृथग्वक्ष्यामि लक्षणम्।
उद्दिष्टानामियथान्यायमुदाहरणमेव च॥ ११॥

स्वराणां संकेता यथा—

अ॑	उदात्तः
अ॒	अनुदात्तः
अ॑	उदात्तात् परः स्वरितः
अँ	जात्यः स्वरितः

काठकसंहितायां स्वरविचारणा ।

काठकसंहितायां— उदात्तोऽनुदात्तः स्वरितः प्रचयश्चेति चातुःस्वर्यमेवाधीयतेऽध्येतृभिः । तत्र स्वरितः शुद्धो जात्यश्चेति द्विरूपः । उदात्तात्परः स्वरूपेणानुदात्तकः शुद्धः स्वरितः । अनुदात्तात्परः, पदादिर्वा, स्वरूपेणोभयरूपः, उदात्ततुल्यः, स्वयं स्वरितश्च जात्यः स्वरितः । कम्पो नास्त्येव । स्वरितात्पूर्व उदात्तः स्वरितात्परः प्रचयः । प्रचयश्चोदात्ते परेऽनुदात्तो भवति ।

१— काठके तूदात्त ऊर्ध्वं रेखाङ्कितः । यथा—

निं॒ षसा॒द् धृ॒तव्र॑तो॒ वरु॑णः॒ पस्त्या॒स्वा । सा॒म्रा॒ज्या॑य सु॒क्रतुः॑ ।

इति । [काठक सं० ७।१४।८२]

२— अनुदात्तस्वरोऽरेखितः । (पूर्वमेवोदाहरणम् ।)

३— स्वरितोऽधो बिन्दुयुक्तः । यथा— इषे॓ त्वो॓र्जे॓ त्वा॒ ।

४— जात्योऽनुदात्ते परेऽधोऽर्धेव क्रितः । यथा— ' ठ्यु॒ह्यन्महिषो॓ ' ।

उदात्ते परेऽधः कीलाङ्कितो जात्यः । यथा— ' पस्त्या॒स्वा॑ ' ।

५— प्रचयाद्या शेषाः स्वरा रेखाङ्कनवर्जिताः स्युः ।

६— काठकानां ब्राह्मणस्य स्वरास्तु मन्त्रवदेव भवन्ति । नास्ति तेभ्यः कश्चिद्विशेषः । अत्र बीजं च मन्त्रब्राह्मणयोरुभयो-मिश्रतया एकत्र पाठसन्निवेश एवेति । अतएव चोक्तं भगवता कात्यायनेन भाषिकसूत्रे— " मन्त्रस्वरवद्ब्राह्मण-स्वरश्चरकाणाम् " इति । [कात्या० भाषि० सू० ३।१६]

काठकाक्षरका एवेति नाविदितं विदुषामिति दिक् ।

मैत्रायणीय-संहितायां स्वर-विमर्शः ।

मैत्रायणीय-शाखायां तावच्चातुःस्वर्यं मुख्यम् । ते च चत्वारः स्वराः:—
१ उदात्तः, २ अनुदात्तः, ३ स्वरितः, ४ प्रचयः चेति । तत्र स्वरितः सप्तधाऽऽस्ते—
१ जात्यः, २ अभिनिहितः, ३ प्रक्लिष्टः, ४ क्षैप्रः, ५ तैरोव्यञ्जनः, ६ तैरोविरामः, ७ पादवृत्तः, चेति भेदात् ।
तत्र जात्याद्यश्चत्वारः स्वराः प्रकम्पन्तेऽतस्तद्भेदश्चतुर्थो कम्पस्वरः । इति स्वराः ।

स्वरलक्षणानि स्वरलेखन-पद्धतिश्च ।

(१) उच्च उदात्तः:- ऊर्ध्वं रक्तोऽर्थादुद्रेखितश्चोदात्तः । यथा 'प्रं'

(२) नीचोऽनुदात्तः:- नीचरक्तोऽर्थादधोरेखितश्चानुदात्तः । यथा 'चु'

(३) उपरि त्रिधारक्तस्तिर्यग्रक्तो वा (v) स्वरितः । यथा ' सुभूर्तायु कर्मुणा,   स्वः: ' (एष उपरिलिख्यते)

(४) अकम्पस्वरितपरोऽक्षरमध्ये रक्तः प्रचयः । यथा ' र्यम्बकं यजामहे ' (एषोऽक्षरमध्ये लिख्यते)

- Udatta indicated by ◌॑ U+0951 *(note – this is a Svarita in most Veda texts)*

- Anudatta indicated by ◌᳘ U+1CD8

- Svarita indicated by ◌᳕ U+1CD5 *(a variant for ◌᳛ U+1CDB)*

[१४]   मैत्रायणी-संहितायाः ।

(८) उदात्तेकारोकारयोः स्थाने यवयोः परोऽनुदात्तः क्षैप्रः । अथवा—
इ उ स्थाने यवौ जायेते उच्चयोस्तयोः । ताभ्यामुभयतः स्वारः क्षैप्र इत्यभिधीयते ॥
यथा— युयोध्युस्मत्, न्विन्द्रम् ।

(९) उदात्तपूर्वं यत्किञ्चिच्छन्दासि स्वरितं भवेत् । एष सर्वैर्बहुस्वारस्तैरोव्यञ्जन एव च ॥
यथा— केतवो विरुश्मयो जनं अनु ।

- Svarita after Udatta indicated by ◌᳖ U+1CD6

89

अत्र खरचिह्वान्यक्षराणामुरसि वा सिरसि वारोहन्ति । तानि तथैव मुद्रापयितुम-
शक्यानि, तादृगायसाक्षराणामभावात् । अतोऽधोलिखितानि खरचिह्वानि मैत्रायणी-
संहिताया मुद्रणार्थं संकल्प्यन्ते । यथा—

$$त्वॅ \quad = \quad त्वा$$

$$यॅ \quad = \quad यॅ$$

$$जु \quad = \quad जु$$

For the sake of proper printing the Svarita accents used are

- Svarita indicated by ◌ U+1CD6 (to mean ◌ U+1CD4)

- Svarita indicated by ◌ U+1CD5 (to mean ◌ U+1CDB)

- Svarita indicated by ◌ U+1CD8 (to mean ◌ U+1CD7)

B. The *accentuation* of the *Vájasaneyi-samhitá* is in general the same as that of the *Rik*-Sanhitá, besides some particularities regarding the *Svarita*. —

1. At the beginning of the verse the *unaccented* syllables, till the first accented one, are denoted by horizontal strokes beneath them: परमे, पृथिविसत्, व्रतारिद्वासत्, हेमन्तशिशिरौ, त्रिणवत्रयस्त्रिंशौ.

2. The *udátta* is denoted by an horizontal stroke beneath the preceding *unaccented* syllable, and by a perpendicular one above the following *unaccented* syllable नृषदम्, either of these strokes being of course wanting, if there is no preceding (पतिः) or no following syllable (नृषत्), or if the preceding (यः पतिः) or the following syllable (नृषद्येषाम्, मह्यो ये धनम्, पर्णा न वेरनु, युक्त्वा हि ये तवाश्वासः) is an accented one. — The perpendicular stroke is changed into an horizontal one, if the next following syllable is accented नृषद् यः. —

3. The *svarita* has various forms: *a*. at the *beginning* of the verse: before an unaccented syllable कोऽसि — before an accented one: 1) before an udátta गोऽसौ च. 2) before a svarita घ्रा स्वः: — if it stands alone घ्रा. —

b. after an *unaccented* syllable: before an unaccented one आस्येन (आस्येन in the Kânva-Çâkhâ): — before an accented one: 1) before an udátta आस्ये यासाम् (आस्ये यासाम् in the Kânva-Çâkhâ). 2) before a svarita? (I do not remember having found an instance of this case): — at the end आस्ये. —

c. after an *accented* syllable: I) after an udátta: before an unaccented syllable परमे व्योमन्: — before an accented one: 1) before an udátta पृढात्स्वर्ज्यातिः: 2) before a svarita? — at the end परमः स्वः. — II) after a svarita: before an unaccented syllable घ्रा स्वरसि — before an udátta or svarita? — at the end घ्रा स्वः. —

Vedic Characters & Symbols

While reading Vedic Texts, we notice some letters, characters and symbols that are in addition to the standard Sanskrit Alphabet. These characters are the accent marks, additional letters and punctuations, that are common in Vedic Sanskrit but rare in classical Sanskrit.

These extend the Sanskrit Alphabet, and only then can it be termed complete. This is necessary to enable reading, writing, typing and proper chanting, and thus correctly understanding the rich Vedic heritage of India.

In the olden days, the Veda was passed on from father to son or in a gurukul from master to disciple in an oral tradition. When handwritten scripts appeared, then special signs and symbols were devised to augment the Sanskrit Alphabet so that written Sanskrit remained true to the spoken. When printing presses began and books began to appear in print, there was some transition or variation in the way the augmented symbols were put in print in different presses. Some symbols also got lost from handwriting to printing, while some new symbols got added.

Each ashram and gurukul and pundit or scholarly reader needs to be aware of the tone and pitch during recitation and chanting of the Vedas. Even university professors and researchers delving into the Vedas need to be aware of the correct meaning and application of these verses. Furthermore, as we move from offset printing and metal type setting to the computer and smartphone era, this book serves as an invaluable resource.

These additional letters, characters and symbols are:

Symbol	Name	Occurs in	Remarks, Example
ळ	Consonant Heavy lla, enunciated with a rolled tongue as "lda"	Rigveda, Kanva Shukla Yajurveda	A consonant that appears due to sandhi. Change of letter ड to ळ in specific instances. अग्निमीळे पुरोहितं RV 1.1.1.1
ळ्ह	A sandhi Consonant ळ ੍ ह = ळ्ह	Rigveda	A consonant that appears due to sandhi. Change of letter ढ to ळ्ह in specific instances. दृळ्हा वि RV 1.7.34.12
य	Consonant Heavy yya, enunciated as "ज ja"	Shukla Yajurveda. E.g. Rudra ashtadhyayi	A consonant that appears due to sandhi. Change of letter य to य in specific instances. यज्जाग्रति SYV 16.5
॑	Svarita accent	Rigveda, Yajurveda, Atharvaveda	In most manuscripts it is a Svarita. गणपतिꣳ हवामहे KYV (However in the Kathaka Samhita it is an Udatta)

	Anudatta accent	Rigveda, Yajurveda, Atharvaveda	In most manuscripts it is an Anudatta. गण॒पति॑ꣳ हवामहे KYV (However in the Kathaka Samhita it is a Jatya Svarita that follows an anudatta)
	Tone "karshana"	Samaveda गान singing version	Generally seen above numeral २ , where २ indicates a pluta or extra long chant. स्या॒रिता२३४ SAMA SINGING
	Tone "prenkha"	Samaveda गान singing version	Generally seen above numeral २ , where २ indicates a pluta or extra long chant. तोया॒रइ I SAMA SINGING
//	Punctuation "Nih-Shvasa"	Samaveda गान singing version	Short pause to take breath माऽ३साऽ५इ ॑क्ताऽ ६५६: II SAMA SINGING

	Accent "midline svarita"		These two accent marks are the same. Variant by different printing presses. ॐ इषे॑ त्वा or ॐ इषे॑ त्वा॒ MAITRAYANI SAMHITA
	Small-omega Svarita accent	 	These accent marks are the same. Variant by different printing presses. It is a जात्य Jatya Svarita that follows an Udatta. ॐ इषे॑ त्वा सुभूतायँ॒ or ॐ इषे॑ त्वा॒ सुभूताय॒ MAITRAYANI SAMHITA 1.1.1
	L Svarita accent		These two accent marks are the same. Variant by different printing presses.
	Hook Svarita accent		Variant by different printing presses. ˘ पर्णवती कार्या ˘ MAITRAYANI SAMHITA 4.1.1

	Arc Svarita accent	Shukla Yajurveda, Krishna Yajurveda Maitrayani Samhita	नमस्तेरुद्रमन्यवंडउ RUDRASHTADHYAYI 5.1 देवा VAJASANEYI SAMHITA 17.56 पर्णवती कार्या MAITRAYANI SAMHITA 4.1.1
	Caret-below Svarita accent		Variant mark by another printing press. प्रसवेऽश्विनो Schroeder प्रसवेऽश्विनो Satvalekar Krishna Yajurveda KATHAKA SAMHITA 1.2
	Short Kampa accent	Rigveda, Atharvaveda	Short vowel sandhi Kampa व्य१श्थिनः RIGVEDA 1.9.48.6
	Long Kampa accent	Rigveda, Atharvaveda	Long vowel sandhi Kampa पस्त्या३स्वा RIGVEDA 1.6.25.10

Symbol	Name	Occurs in	Example
◌̎	Dirgha Svarita accent	Rudram Namakam from Krishna Yajurveda.	Long svarita, to be chanted in high pitch for longer duration before reducing pitch मीढुषे̎ । NAMAKAM 1
◌	Triple-bar Svarita accent		These two accent marks are the same. Variant by different printing presses.
◌	bar-below Anudatta accent	Atharvaveda Paippalada Samhita	पावुका॒ PAIPPALADA SAMHITA 1.25.1
◌	dot-below Svarita Accent	Atharvaveda Paippalada Samhita	गर्भे̇ PAIPPALADA SAMHITA 1.25.1

	two-dots-below Accent	द्वि॒त एकत॒ः SATAPATHA BRAHMANA 1.2.2.15 Ajmer द्वि॒त एकत॒ः SATAPATHA BRAHMANA 1.2.2.15 Weber	Variant mark by a printing press. हि॒ यज्ञम् ॥१ SATAPATHA BRAHMANA 1.1.2.23
	three-dots-below Accent		Variant mark by a printing press. हि॒ यज्ञम् ॥१ SATAPATHA BRAHMANA 1.1.2.23
	Standalone Svarita accent	Atharvaveda	तन्वो॒ ꣼ अद्य ATHARVAVEDA SAMHITA 1.1.1.1
	Svarita accent for Visarga	Rudra Ashtadhyayi from Shukla Yajurveda	नम॑ः शिवाय॑ RUDRA ASHTADHYAYI 5.41

	Udatta accent for Visarga	Rudra Ashtadhyayi from Shukla Yajurveda	श्रिताश्सहस्रशो RUDRA ASHTADHYAYI 5.6
	Mirrored Udatta accent for Visarga	Rudra Ashtadhyayi from Shukla Yajurveda	बब्भ्रुःसुमङ्गलः । RUDRA ASHTADHYAYI 5.6
	Anudatta accent for Visarga	Rudra Ashtadhyayi from Shukla Yajurveda	यथानः RUDRA ASHTADHYAYI 5.4
	Mirrored Anudatta accent for Visarga	Rudra Ashtadhyayi from Shukla Yajurveda	नुदहार्य RUDRA ASHTADHYAYI 5.7
	Udatta accent for Visarga (with tail)	Rudra Ashtadhyayi	निषङ्गधिः । RUDRA ASHTADHYAYI 5.10

	Anudatta accent (with tail) for Visarga	Madhyandina Shukla Yajurveda (loose leaf edition)	नमोॅभिः । SHUKLA YAJURVEDA 13.43
	Tiryak	Shukla Yajurveda. E.g. ◌ँ , यँ	Can be attached to gomukhas and nasalized semivowels

	Samaveda accent (zero)	Samaveda Singing	गृणानोॅह
	Samaveda Udatta accent (one)	Samaveda Samhita, Samaveda Singing	अग्न आ SAMAVEDA 1.1 आइन्द्रमर्चं।
	Samaveda Svarita accent (two)	Samaveda Samhita, Samaveda Singing	आइन्द्रमर्चं।

३ ◌	Samaveda Anudatta accent (three)	Samaveda Samhita, Samaveda Singing	अभिप्रवस्सुरा
४ ◌	Samaveda tone (four)	Samaveda Samhita, Samaveda Singing	अभिप्रवस्सुरा
५ ◌	Samaveda tone (five)	Samaveda Samhita, Samaveda Singing	अभिप्रवस्सुरा
अ ◌	Samaveda sign Akara	Samaveda Singing	यथाविदाऽ २३४इ ।
उ ◌	Samaveda accent Ukara	Samaveda Samhita	परो

क ◌	Samaveda accent (kakara)	Samaveda Samhita	तन्वा
न ◌	Samaveda sign Nakara	Samaveda Samhita	ष्णवाऽ३इ ॥
र ◌	Samaveda accent Repha	Samaveda Samhita, Samaveda Singing	होता , अभिप्रवस्सुरा
वि ◌	Samaveda sign Vikara	Samaveda Singing	इन्द्रेऽ२स्सोमाऽ

◌	Nasalization independent candrabindu	Samaveda Singing	सूनुँसत्याऽ

	Nasalization independent candrabindu with tiryak. Chant as "गुँ, gum"	Krishna Yajurveda. E.g. Rudram Namakam, Taittiriya Brahmana	(अनुस्वार + उष्म स्वर) चेमाꣳ रुद्रा SAMHITA 4.5.1 क्षत्रꣳसंघत्तं BRAHMANA 1.1.1
	Nasalization independent anusvara. Chant as "ग्ग्, gg"	Krishna Yajurveda. E.g. Purusha Sukta, Taittiriya Brahmana	(अनुस्वार + संयुक्त उष्म स्वर) अहीꣴ श्व SAMHITA 4.5.1 श्रोत्रꣴ स्थइश्रो BRAHMANA 1.1.4
ˇ	Punctuation small-v to show or insert missing letter(s)	Recent transcribing of ancient documents.	शान्त्यै ̆ पर्णॅवती MAITRAYANI SAMHITA IV.1.1
—	Punctuation Headstroke to show section of manuscript is illegible	Krishna Yajurveda Maitrayani Samhita (Recent transcribing)	योनि ̄ रंदित्या , स्थादि ̄ न्द्रस्य MAITRAYANI SAMHITA 1.1.2

Variant Symbols in Print

Some of the Vedic symbols that mean the same thing are seen shaped variously by different printers or print editions.

౿	Independent long Anusvara (antar-gomukha)	Rudra Ashtadhyayi (Anusvara when facing sibilants श , ष , स , ह , repha र)	धनुष्ट्व౫सहस्त्र RUDRA ASHTADHYAYI 5.13
౿	independent long Anusvara (bahir-gomukha)	Variant by different printing press	Anusvara changes to long धनुष्ट्व౫सहस्त्र RUDRA ASHTADHYAYI 5.13
౿	Standalone long Anusvara (vama-gomukha)	Shukla Yajurveda Vajasaneyi Samhita	धनुष्ट्व౫सहस्त्र VAJASANEYI SAMHITA 16.13
౿	Standalone long Anusvara (vama-gomukha with tail)	Shukla Yajurveda Vajasaneyi Samhita	तेषा౫सहस्त्र VAJASANEYI SAMHITA 16.56

६ं	Standalone long Anusvara	Rudra Ashtadhyayi. धनुष्ट्वँः‌सहस्र RUDRA ASHTADHYAYI 5.13	Anusvara changes to long when facing sibilants श , ष , स , ह , or repha र
६	Standalone long Anusvara	E.g. हिं सीँः to हिंःसीँः RUDRA ASHTADHYAYI 5.3	Anusvara changes to long when facing sibilants श , ष , स , ह , or repha र

The standalone long Anusvaras are usually variants of two types used by different printing presses. The two types indicate
- two different pitch accent sequences or
- whether the following sibilant is a conjunct

ঽं	Standalone long Anusvara	Rudra Ashtadhyayi of Shukla Yajurveda	Variant from another printing press धनुष्ट्वঽःसहस्र RUDRA ASHTADHYAYI 5.13
ঽ	Standalone long Anusvara	Madhyandina Shukla Yajurveda (loose leaf edition)	ऋतुराঽकल्पं SHUKLA YAJURVEDA 13.43

꣹	Dirgha Candrabindu (variant in print for sequence ँ+२)	Shukla Yajurveda Vajasaneyi Samhita	सोम देवो देवाꣴ ॥ ऽउपा SHUKLA YAJURVEDA 5.39
꣹	independent Candrabindu (three)	(variant in print for sequence ँ+३)	विन्दतीꣴ ॥ १ RIGVEDA 10.11.146.1
Note – The symbols ँ , ꣲ , ꣳ , ꣴ may simply be printing limitations in various texts to represent the standard candrabindu ँ U+0901 and not independent symbols to mean anything specific			

Rarely seen Symbols

Some of the Vedic symbols are rare in modern publications. They are from ancient palm leaf texts or other sources that are not commonly available in print.

Symbol	Name	Occurs in	
꣼	Punctuation Flower – a gap filler to show technical verse	Various flower symbols are seen	Pointer to footnote, reference etc.

৩	Punctuation Clip - gap filler	Palm leaf texts	
৩	Punctuation Siddham - to show auspicious verse	Palm leaf texts	
ŝ	Avagraha Candrabindu	Shatarudriya (from Krishna Yajurveda Namakam)	
ꣾ	Samaveda sign Avagraha	Srautakosa (verses for Samaveda Singing)	
प	Samaveda sign Pakara	Srautakosa (verses for Samaveda Singing)	

	Samaveda tone Six	Srautakosa (verses for Samaveda Singing)	
	Punctuation sign Atikrama – to show skipping of a svara pitch	Samaveda Singing. Kauthama Recension. Bengali script	
	Pitch marker Ring	Samaveda Singing. Jaiminiya Recension. Grantha script	
	Pitch marker Double Ring	Samaveda Singing. Jaiminiya Recension. Grantha script	
	Svarita accent	Grantha script of Tamil Nadu used in Krishna Yajurveda	

ಀ	Standalone long Anusvara (antar-gomukha doubled)	Nandinagari script used in South India	
↑	Tone "shara"	Srautakosa (verses for Samaveda Singing)	
⹀	Accent Double Hyphen below		
⹁	Accent Double Arc below		
⹂	Accent Double 3 dots below		

| ॥ | Vedic Timing Double Bars - used generally after numerals 2 and 3 to mean dirgha and pluta resp. | Samaveda Singing, Satapatha Brahmana | Double danda that is not a full stop Virama |

Devanagari Fonts with Vedic Extensions

Advaita Sanskrit

Sanskrit2020

https://sourceforge.net/projects/advaita-sharada-font/

Adishila

https://adishila.com/fonts/

Sanskrit Text – a font that ships with Windows 10.

Shobhika

https://ctan.org/tex-archive/fonts/shobhika?lang=en

Siddhanta

http://svayambhava.blogspot.com/p/siddhanta-devanagariunicode-open-type.html

Praja

http://www.peterffreund.com/Resources/Resource_Page.html

Sanskrit Pro

https://www.sanskritpro.com/

Noto Sans Devanagari

https://www.google.com/get/noto/#sans-deva

Keyboard IME for Vedic Extensions

IME keyboard Sanskrit2020A

https://sourceforge.net/projects/advaita-sharada-font/files/Devanagari/

Vidyut keyboard

http://www.mywhatever.com/sanskrit/vidyut/

http://www.peterffreund.com/Resources/Resource_Page.html

for Online or browser typing
https://www.lexilogos.com/keyboard/sanskrit_vedic.htm

https://help.keyman.com/keyboard/itrans_devanagari_sanskrit_vedic/1.0.0/itrans_devanagari_sanskrit_vedic

Unicode for Vedic Extensions

Unicode Block Devanagari 0900 to 09FF
https://unicode.org/charts/PDF/U0900.pdf

Unicode Block Vedic Extensions 1CD0 to 1CFF
https://unicode.org/charts/PDF/U1CD0.pdf

Unicode Block Devanagari Extended A8E0 to A8FF
https://unicode.org/charts/PDF/UA8E0.pdf

Unicode for South and Central Asia scripts
https://www.unicode.org/versions/Unicode13.0.0/ch12.pdf

Vedic Swastika – auspiciousness sign is available in the Unicode Tibetan character set

https://unicode.org/charts/PDF/U0F00.pdf

https://unicode-table.com/en/blocks/tibetan/

https://home.unicode.org/

Glossary

अक्षर — syllable, alphabet, letter, e.g. अ phoneme
अघोष वर्ण — unvoiced consonant e.g. क, ख, श, ष , स, ह
अणु — ¼ मात्रा काल Enunciated for a length of a quarter matra time period.
अनुदात्त — low pitch
अनुनासिका — Anunāsikā i.e. Nasalized, mouth along with nose
अनुस्वार — ं Anusvāra अं
अन्तःस्थ — य् र् ल् व् the semivowel letters, also known as **liquid** letters, letters intermediate between vowels and consonants
अयोगवाह — ँ ं ः ᳵ ᳶ ꣳ ꣴ candrabindu, Anusvāra, Visarga, Ardha Visarga, Jihvāmūlīya, Upadhmānīya, Yama, Nāsikya, Svarabhakti. A dependent letter arising out of vowel sandhi.
अवग्रह — ऽ Avagraha, indicates elision of the vowel अ or आ
उच्चारण — Enunciation
उदात्त — normal pitch
ऊष्म — श् ष् स् the sibilant letters, also called **spirants** or **fricatives**. The hissing sounds.
ऋग्वेद प्रातिशाख्य — Rigved Pratisakhya, a text dealing with letters and phonetics
गुरु स्वर — a syllable of two or more matras, e.g. long vowel आ, conjunct consonant श्र
घोष वर्ण — voiced
तैत्तिरीय प्रातिशाख्य — Taittiriya Pratisakhya, a text dealing with letters and phonetics
दीर्घ — आ ई ऊ ॠ ए ऐ ओ औ long vowels and syllables, e.g. का, के Take double the time of speaking compared to the short vowels.
नासिक्य — हुँ / हूँ sound. An ayogavaha

परमाणु — 1/8 मात्रा काल Time period half of Aṇu
पाणिनीय शिक्षा — Paniniya Siksha, a text dealing with alphabets and phonetics
प्रातिशाख्य — Pratisakhya is an ancient text dealing with the letters and phonetics of the Sanskrit language
प्लुत — Pluta vowel. Elongation in time of speaking e.g. अ३ , ई३ etc. Used also when calling someone from a distance.
मात्रा — Time taken to utter a letter. A consonant takes half matra time period, whereas a short vowel takes one matra time period. Also called Mora. Alternate meaning is the vowel symbol.
यम — कुँ, खुँ, गुँ, घुँ sounds. गुँ is written as ꣡,꣢ Ayogavaha
लघु स्वर — a syllable of one matra, e.g. short vowel अ
वर्ग — row class consonant letters, these are 25
वर्ण — letter of the alphabet
वाजसनेयी प्रातिशाख्य — Vajasneyi Pratisakhya, a text dealing with letters and phonetics
विसर्जनीय — ः Visarga विसर्ग अः
वैदिक — Vedic Sanskrit of the ancient texts
व्यञ्जन — consonant
संयुक्त अक्षर — conjunct consonant, e.g. क्त
सन्ध्यक्षर, सन्धि अक्षर — ए ऐ ओ औ the diphthong vowel letters
स्पर्श वर्ण — contacted letter, a consonant known as a **plosive**
स्फोटन — sphoṭana — when a consonant is followed by a letter of the कवर्ग then a natural gap in enunciation occurs
स्वर — vowel. Also means accent on vowel e.g. Anudata
स्वरित — high pitch
ह्रस्व — अ इ उ ऋ ऌ the short vowels and syllables, e.g. क, कि etc.

References

Author	Title	Year	Ed	Publisher
V S Apte	संस्कृत हिन्दी कोश (1890 Ed)	1997	1st	Oriental Book Center, Delhi
Dr. Somlekha	पाणिनीय शिक्षा	2014	1st	Chaukhamba Sanskrit Pratishthan, Delhi
Shivraj Acharya Kondinyayan	पाणिनीय शिक्षा	2012	1st	Chaukhamba Surbharti Prakashan, Varanasi
Yudhisthir Mimamsak	शिक्षा सूत्राणि	2014	1st	Ram Lal Kapoor Trust, Sonipat
Shriram Sharma Acharya	ऋग्वेद संहिता	2005	1st	Yugnirman Yojana, Mathura
Dr. R. L. Kashyap	ऋग्वेद मन्त्र संहिता Rig Veda Mantra Samhita	2003	1st	Sri Aurobindo Kapali Shastry Institute of Vedic Culture, Bangalore
Manomohan Ghosh	Paniniya Siksa	1938	1st	University of Calcutta, Calcutta
Radheyshyam Khemka	शुक्ल यजुर्वेदीय रुद्राष्टाध्यायी	2016	1st	Gita Press, Gorakhpur
Thomas Egenes	Introduction to Sanskrit - Part Two	2000	1st	Motilal Banarsidass, Delhi
Pushpa Dikshit	अष्टाध्यायी सूत्रपाठः	2010	1st	Samskrita Bharati, New Delhi

Author	Title	Year	Edition	Publisher
Acharya Swami Vijayanand Puri	तैत्तिरीयोपनिषत्	1999	1st	Kailash Ashram, Rishikesh
Rajendralala Mitra	तैत्तिरीयप्रातिशाख्यं त्रिभाष्यरत्ननाम टीकासहितम्	1872	1st	Asiatic Society of Bengal, Calcutta
K. Rangacharya and R. Shama Sastri	तैत्तिरीयप्रातिशाख्यम् सोमयार्यविरचित त्रिभाष्यरत्नाख्य व्याख्यया गार्ग्यगोपालयज्वविरचित वेदिकाभरणाख्य व्याख्यया च सहितम्	1906	1st	Government Oriental Library, Mysore
William D. Whitney	The Taittiriya Pratisakhya with its commentary the Tribhashyaratna (1868 Ed)	1973	1st	Motilal Banarsidass , Delhi
William Dwight Whitney	A Sanskrit Grammar, Including both the classical language, and the older dialects, of veda and brahmana	1879	1st	Leipzig, Breitkopf and Hārtel
C. C. Uhlenbeck	A Manual of Sanskrit Phonetics	1898	1st	Uhlenbeck, London
Charles Wikner	A Practical Sanskrit Introductory	1996	1st	Charles Wikner, South Africa
Ashwini Kumar Aggarwal	Rudra Puja	2016	1st	Zorba Books, Gurgaon
Ashwini Kumar Aggarwal	The Sanskrit Alphabet	2017	1st	Devotees of Sri Sri Ravi Shankar Ashram, Punjab
	Sanskrit Sandhi Handbook	2019	1st	

Unicode Status (Vedic)

https://scriptsource.org/cms/scripts/page.php?item_id=entry_detail&uid=nb2xvfymgv

https://unicode.org/charts/nameslist/n_1CD0.html

Leopold Von Schroeder - मैत्रायणी संहिता Vol4 - 1st – 1886 – F A Brockhaus, Leipzig

Leopold Von Schroeder - काठकं संहिता Vol1 - 1st – 1900 – F A Brockhaus, Leipzig

Satyavrat Sama - Sayanacharya सामवेद संहिता तत्र छन्दआर्ब्विकः Vol1 - 1st – 1871 to 1878 Reprint 1983 – Munshiram Manoharlal Publishers, New Delhi

A. Mahadeva Sastri - तैत्तिरीय ब्राह्मणम् Vol1 - 1st – 1908 – Maharaja of Mysore, Mysore

Arthur Anthony Macdonell – A Vedic Grammar for Students - 1st - 1916 – Oxford University Press, London

Shripad Damodar Satvalekar – अथर्व वेद का स्वाध्याय - 1st - 1918 – Sarasvati Ashram, Lahore

Raghu Vira – अथर्ववेदीया पैप्पलाद संहिता Vol1 - 1st - 1936 – The International Academy of Indian Culture, Lahore

Sayanacharya & Hari Swami – वाजसनेयि माध्यन्दिन शतपथ ब्राह्मणम् Vol1 - 1st - 1939 – Nag Publishers, Delhi

Vinayak Ganesh Apte – कृष्ण यजुर्वेदीय तैत्तिरीय संहिता Vol1 - 1st - 1940 – Anandashram, Pune

Shripad Damodar Satvalekar - यजुर्वेदीय मैत्रायणी संहिता - 1st - 1942 - Satvalekar, Satara

Shripad Damodar Satvalekar – यजुर्वेदीय काठक संहिता - 1st - 1942 - Satvalekar, Satara

Shripad Damodar Satvalekar – यजुर्वेदीय काण्व संहिता - 1st - 1942 - Satvalekar, Satara

Shripad Damodar Satvalekar – सामवेद संहिता – 3rd - 1956 – Swadhyay Mandal, Pardi

माध्यन्दिनीये शतपथ ब्राह्मणम् – 1st - 1950 – Vedic Yantralaya, Ajmer

Yudhisthir Mimansak – वैदिक स्वर मिमांसा – 1st - 1958 - Reprint 2009 – Ramlal Kapoor Trust, Sonipat

Ramamurthi Shrouthi- सामवेदः ऊहऊह्यगानम् - 1st - 1966 – Sri Sharada Peetham, Sringeri

Brij Bihari Chaubey - वैदिक स्वर बोध –1972 – Reprint 2004 – Katyayan Vaidik Sahitya Prakashan, Hoshiarpur

Vamdev Mishra - स्वर प्रक्रिया प्रकाश - 1st - 1999 - Chaukhamba Vidyabhawan, Varanasi

Gopalchandra Mishra - सम्प्रदाय प्रबोधिनी शिक्षा – 1st – 1999 - Chaukhamba Vidya Bhawan, Varanasi

Gopalchandra Mishra - माध्यन्दिनीय यजुर्वेद एवं सामवेद की पाठ परम्परा – Benaras Hindu University
http://vedicheritage.gov.in/hi/samhitas/yajurveda/vajasneyi-madhyandina-samhita/

शुक्ल यजुर्वेद माध्यंदिनीय संहिता – Loose Leaf Edition – 2010 - Khemraj Shrikrishnadas, Mumbai

Dharmendra Kumar & Pradyumnachandra ऋग्वेद संहिता – 1st – 2013 – Delhi Sanskrit Academy, New Delhi

Taittiriya Brahmana
https://archive.org/details/in.gov.ignca.7919/page/n31/mode/2up

From the Net

http://sanskritdictionary.com/ Sanskrit online dictionary
http://spokensanskrit.de/ Spoken Sanskrit online dictionary
http://www.sanskritsounds.com/ Sanskrit Sounds by Nikolai Bachman
http://www.aa.tufs.ac.jp/~tjun/sktdic/ Apte Sanskrit English -
Takashima's Labo
http://www.tilakpyle.com/sanskrit.htm Sanskrit Pronunciation Guide
https://swadhyaymandal.org.in/ Swadhyay Mandal, Killa Pardi, Surat
https://www.facebook.com/VaidikaSamshodhanMandal/ Vaidika
Samshodhana Mandala, Pune
https://en.wikipedia.org/wiki/Sri_Venkateswar_Steam_Press Khemraj
Shrikrishnadas Shri Venkateshwar Press, Mumbai
http://www.aanandashram-sanstha.org/Manuscripts.html Anandashram,
Pune
http://www.paropkarinisabha.com/ Vedic Yantralaya, Ajmer

Audio Learning

Vyoma Linguistics Labs Foundation, Bangalore http://www.vyomalabs.in/

Epilogue

The ॐ symbol is created from three parts, namely the "3" shape of अ, the knob from ऊ , and the candrabindu ँ that is used to indicate a nasalized vowel. In other words, Sattva Rajas Tamas, or the Trinity that supports creation.

सर्वे भवन्तु सुखिनः । सर्वे सन्तु निरामयाः ।

सर्वे भद्राणि पश्यन्तु । मा कश्चिद् दुःख भाग् भवेत् ॥

ॐ शान्तिः शान्तिः शान्तिः

When faith has blossomed in life, Every step is led by the Divine.

Sri Sri Ravi Shankar

Om Namah Shivaya

जय गुरुदेव